D1297145
DELTA
TARGET CENTER
ASG CLOSED CAPTIONING

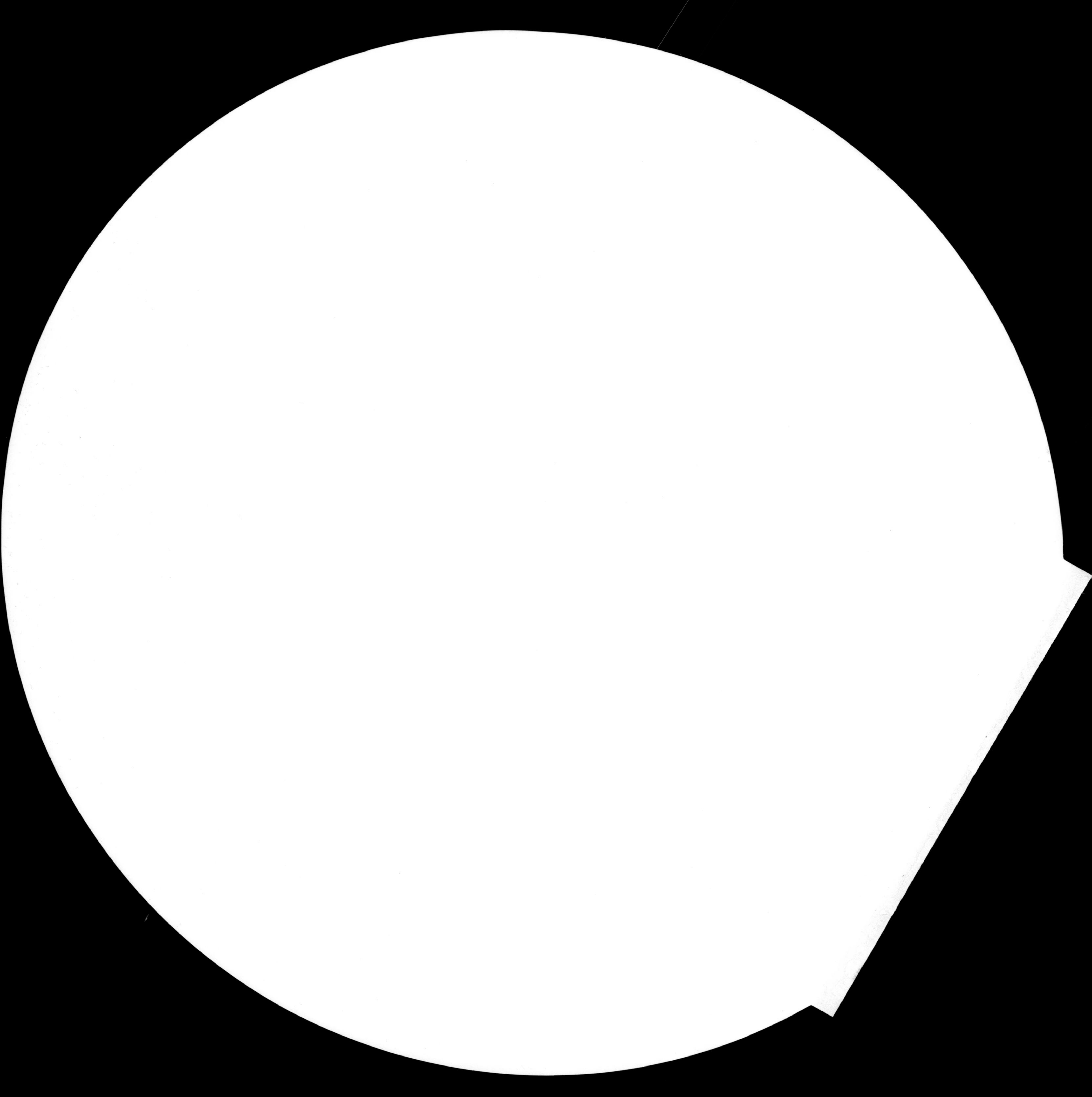

Baseball

RUCKUS
BOOKS

ISBN 978-1-9264440-3-1

Design: Compass Creative Studio Inc.
Author: Christopher Kubala

The author and publisher have made every effort to ensure the information contained in this book was correct at the time of going to press and accept no responsibility for any loss, injury or inconvenience sustained by any person using this book.

All Images: Getty Images
Editor: Faeryn Genovese

TABLE OF CONTENTS

HISTORY OF MAJOR LEAGUE BASEBALL

GREATEST PLAYERS

MAJOR LEAGUE TEAMS

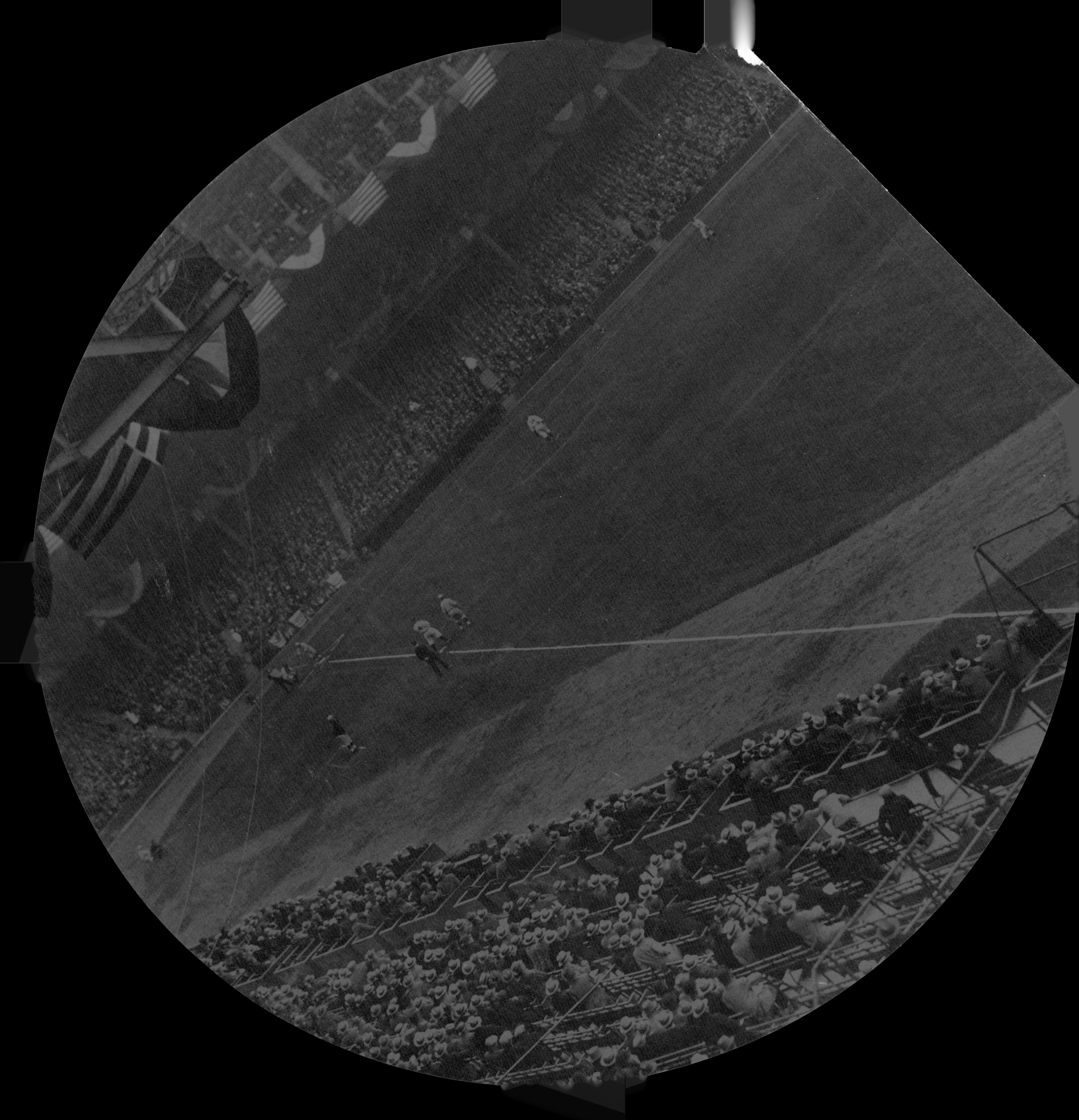

THE HISTORY OF

MAJOR LEAGUE BASEBALL

THE HISTORY OF
MAJOR LEAGUE BASEBALL

The history of baseball as we know it today dates back nearly two centuries. The first official rules written for the sport came in 1845 for a team in New York City known as the Knickerbockers. The rules were written by Shane Ryley Foster, who some consider to be the "father of baseball." Alexander Cartwright, who was the founder of the Knickerbockers franchise, also umpired the first officially recorded game in United States baseball history. He has been credited with introducing the game in small towns and cities across the country as he made his way west for the Gold Rush. The Knickerbockers played the first organized game against the New York Nine on June 19, 1846, on the Elysian Fields in Hoboken, New Jersey. The Knickerbockers chose this venue due to the lack of soft ground to play in the borough of Manhattan. The New York Nine pummeled the Knickerbockers on that afternoon by a score of 23-1. The Knickerbocker rules, as they were known, became rapidly adopted by teams in the New York area, and that version of baseball became known as the "New York Game."

One of the major rule changes that came into play under Cartwright's jurisdiction was one that banned fielders from retiring a hitter or base runner by throwing the ball at them. This action, known as "plugging" or "soaking," was controversial when it was in effect and led to arguments and brawls between teams on a regular basis. Another rule that went into play was that a ball knocked out of the field, or outside the range of first and third base, was foul. While a ball hit outside first and third bases is still foul today, a ball that is in fair territory and leaves the ball park is now a home run.

Other rules that have been changed include one stating that a ball caught on the first bounce is an out (this was changed in 1865), and another that foul balls did not count as strikes (this was changed in 1858, when the rule was altered to state that balls that are fouled off are strikes unless there are two strikes on the batter). In the early days of baseball, the ball had to be pitched underhand, almost like a horseshoe would be tossed. It was not until the 1884 season that overhand pitching was allowed. One rule that was changed quickly stipulated that the winning team had to score 21 runs; it didn't matter how many innings were played as long as a team reached the required 21-run mark.

The Atwater Base Ball Club poses in their home town of Westfield, MA around 1858.

THE BEGINNINGS OF PRO BASEBALL

Professional baseball got its start in 1857, when 16 teams in the New York area sent delegates to a convention. The premise of the convention was to standardize the rules of the sport, and it promoted a revision of the Knickerbocker Rules. The group formed the National Association of Base Ball Players, or NABBP, which was the governing body of the sport from 1857 to 1870. They did not oversee any actual games of their own. By 1862, some teams were offering games to the general public at ballparks and charged admission fees to see the game.

The NABBP expanded over the following years, reaching nearly 100 teams by 1865 due to a burst of popularity during the Civil War. Soldiers from all across the country were playing together, which helped lead to a more cohesive, unified version of the game rather than a mismatch of rules depending on the location. By the time 1867 rolled around, that number was up over the 400-mark and covered the entire country. There were teams from Louisiana to California and all points in between.

The Brooklyn Athletics were one of the biggest powerhouse teams during the NABBP era, claiming seven titles. The team is considered to be the first true dynasty in the history of the sport, but the New York Mutuals were also one of the best teams in the era. The Chicago White Stockings, who would go on to become the Chicago Cubs, won the championship in 1870. The franchise is the oldest team that exists in American organized sports.

The NABBP allowed teams to use professional players beginning in 1869. This came into effect after an 1866 investigation found that Athletic of Philadelphia had paid three players to play on the team. There was no punishment levied to either the team or the respective players, and it was suspected that star players on several teams received compensation even earlier than that. In December 1868 the NABBP instituted a professional category for teams that paid their players.

The Cincinnati Red Stockings were the first team in history to declare themselves professional and by the time the 1869 season began, a dozen teams had declared their professional status. Most of these were among the most successful clubs in the league, so it came as no surprise that they were paying players. The Red Stockings were notorious for procuring the best talent and were extremely proactive in signing available talent. The NABBP had professional players in the ranks alongside the amateurs for just two seasons; after the White Stockings claimed the 1870 championship, dissension was on the rise and times were about to change.

The NABBP split into two groups following the 1870 season, creating the National Association of Professional Baseball Players as a splinter of the amateur ranks. The National Association, as it was known, existed from 1871 to 1875. The White Stockings and the Boston Red Stockings (who had moved from Cincinnati after the 1870 season) were among the charter members of the league. The amateur division of the NABBP disbanded and all but disappeared within a few seasons. Meanwhile, the National Association proved to be ineffective and would be gone after the 1875 season. It was replaced by what is known today as the National League.

The Red Stocking Base Ball Club of Cincinnati, OH poses for a team photo on the field in Cleveland with the Forest City Base Ball Club.

The Chicago White Stockings team pose for a team portrait in 1886. Cap Anson, front, John Clarkson, front row, third from left, King Kelly, front row, far left, and Billy Sunday, back row, far left, are the stars of the team.

THE NATIONAL LEAGUE FORMS: 1876

As the National Association proved to be ineffective for a myriad of reasons, William Hurlbert, who was the financial backer for the White Stockings, devised the National League. The league was team-focused rather than player-focused, and teams were able to enforce the contracts that players signed to prevent them from jumping from team to team based on the highest offer during the season.

Gambling was curtailed as much as possible. There had been concerns that some of the games in previous seasons and leagues may have been determined by methods other than play on the field. This put the validity of results in doubt, which in turn impacted the league's bottom line as far as attendance and revenue streams were concerned. Another major issue that plagued the National Association during its run was teams were forced to play their entire schedule of games even after they were out of contention for the league championship. The largest problem, however, was the gentleman's agreement between all of the teams in the league to only admit Caucasian players. This agreement led to talented players like Moses Fleetwood Walker being dropped from major league rosters and would remain in effect until 1947, when second baseman Jackie Robinson broke the color barrier and suited up for the Brooklyn Dodgers.

The National League did have to contend with several worthy competitors for its stature as the premier major league for baseball in the country. The biggest threat was the American Association, which existed from 1881 through 1891. That league's champions met the National League champion for several years in what was the first attempt at today's World Series. The franchise now known as the Pittsburgh Pirates left the American Association in 1886 to join the National League, the first of several teams to jump leagues. After the 1889 season, the Dodgers and Cincinnati Reds franchises also joined the National League. Then in 1891, after the American Association had folded, the St. Louis Cardinals, who were then known as the Browns, made the jump.

THE AMERICAN LEAGUE BECOMES A MAJOR LEAGUE: 1901

After the dissolution of the American Association, the biggest threat to the National League as a major league in professional baseball was the Western League. The Western League had several starts and stops, going under after the 1885 season, then partway through 1888 and again in June 1893. On November 20, 1893, the Western League reformed for the final time and has been in existence ever since. That day, the league named Ban Johnson as its president after he was elected to the position.

The Western League added another key cornerstone following the 1894 season when Charles Comiskey, who had been involved with Cincinnati in the National League as the club's manager, had his contract expire. Comiskey's playing days had come and gone and rather than continue managing, he decided to see if he would have the same success owning a club. He promptly bought the Sioux City Cornhuskers, moved the team to St. Paul, Minnesota, and renamed the franchise the Saints in time for the 1895 season. He would move the team again in 1900 to Chicago and rename it the White Stockings, later shortened to the White Sox.

The league originally consisted of the Detroit Tigers, the Cornhuskers, the Milwaukee Brewers, the Grand Rapids Rustlers, the Kansas City Blues, the Toledo White Stockings, the Minneapolis Millers and the Indianapolis Indians. Of those teams, only the Tigers stayed in the same city with the same name during the league's existence. The rest of the teams involved created a litany of travel and altered franchises. The Cornhuskers went to Minnesota, and then to Chicago under Comiskey's ownership. The Brewers would become the Baltimore Orioles in 1902 and evolved into the St. Louis Browns in 1904.

Meanwhile, the Rustlers moved to Cleveland in 1900, changing their name to the Cleveland Blues. They would become the Cleveland Broncos in 1902 and the Naps in 1903 before finally settling on the Indians in 1915. The Kansas City Blues relocated to Washington, D.C., and became the Senators in 1900. The team would remain there until the 1961 season when they became the Minnesota Twins. Toledo moved their franchise to Columbus and became the Buckeyes in 1896 before folding up after the 1898 season. They were replaced by the Buffalo Bisons, who would be dropped from the league in 1901 for the newly formed Boston Red Sox, who were called the Americans at the time. The Indianapolis and Minnesota franchises were dropped in 1901 as well.

The Western League changed its name to the American League in a meeting held in Chicago on October 11, 1899. It remained a minor league in the 1900 season, though the National League did grant permission to put a team in Chicago. Comiskey moved his club from St. Paul to the south side of Chicago and the name of the team became the White Stockings. At the same time, the Grand Rapids franchise was shuffled to Cleveland. Another major coup for the fledgling American League came when the National League announced it was dropping Cleveland, Baltimore, Louisville and Washington from its lineup for the 1900 season, opening those cities up.

Following the 1900 season, the American League made the bold move to end its membership with the National Agreement and declare itself a major league. The American League made its first stand as a major league in 1901 and almost immediately started raiding National League rosters in an effort to procure talent. On January 29, 1901, the vote was made by the owners of the league to drop Minnesota, Indianapolis and Buffalo from the ranks while awarding franchises to Boston, Baltimore and Philadelphia. Comiskey's White Stockings claimed the final pennant in the league's history as a minor league when they captured the flag in 1900.

Elmer Flick, outfielder for the Cleveland Blues, takes some swings before a game in New York at Hilltop Park.

COEXISTENCE AND THE FORMATION OF THE WORLD SERIES: 1903

The formation of the American League as a major league and the subsequent raiding of National League franchises created ill will between the owners of the National League and the upstart American League. There was plenty of bitterness and heated contention between the two sides. At first, the National League refused to recognize the existence of the American League but in the end, after nearly two years of back-and-forth between the two sides, cooler heads finally prevailed.

The two sides came to terms on a revised National Agreement. This meant that each side recognized the other as a full-fledged major league. It also meant that each league understood and accepted the other league as an equal partner in dealings and that teams had to respect the contracts that were struck between teams in the other league and their players. The revised agreement also called for the playing of a series between the National League and American League pennant winners in what was called the World Series.

In 1903 things went about as smoothly as could be expected given the built-up animosity between the two leagues in 1901 and 1902. The first World Series game in major league history took place on October 1, 1903, in Boston, as the Boston Americans hosted the Pittsburgh Pirates in the first game of a best-of-nine series. What is interesting to note about the 1903 World Series is that it was contested voluntarily between the two teams and was not mandated by the two leagues. This bit of information would prove to be key the next season.

The Pirates were victorious in Game One, beating Cy Young and the Americans by a score of 7-3. In the end, it would be the Americans who would prevail in the series, five games to three, mainly due to better pitching depth. While Boston had Cy Young, Bill Dineen and Tom Hughes, all of whom won at least 20 games on the season, Pittsburgh was limited as far as pitchers. Sam Leever injured his shoulder trap shooting before the series began, which left Deacon Phillipe to do the heavy lifting on the mound for the Pirates. Philippe threw five complete games and recorded the three Pittsburgh victories, but it was not enough and Boston prevailed. The win for the American League served notice to the National League clubs that the difference in talent between the two leagues was slim.

MCGRAW REFUSES TO PLAY IN WORLD SERIES, CHICAGO DOMINANCE: 1904-1910

While both the Americans and Pirates agreed to take part in the 1903 World Series, the two leagues didn't have that same sort of cooperation a year later. The Americans defended

Half-length portrait of Hall of Famer Cy (Denton True) Young, pitcher for the Boston American League team, standing by grandstand concourse netting at South Side Park, Chicago, IL, 1903.

their American League pennant in 1904, claiming the flag by 1.5 games after going 95-59 on the season. On the other side in the National League, the New York Giants ripped off 106 victories and rolled to a 13-game lead in the final standings to claim the pennant. This would set up a World Series between the Giants and the Americans.

Unfortunately, that series never took place. Giants manager John McGraw had bad blood with Ban Johnson, the president of the American League. McGraw had taken nearly half of the roster of the Baltimore Orioles franchise with him from the American League to the Giants of the National League in July 1902. That was cause for controversy and open hostility between McGraw and Johnson, and their disdain carried over into the potential World Series matchup. The Giants made overtures as early as July 1904 that they did not want to play the American League pennant winner in the World Series. McGraw stated that he had no interest in playing whoever won the pennant. He went on to claim that the Giants were already world champions because they claimed the pennant in the "only real major league." The decision to not play was in defiance of the revised National Agreement made before the 1904 season. When the season ended and the Americans rallied with victories in three of their final four games to claim the American League flag over the New York Highlanders, the Giants were true to their word and did not take part.

Surprised and a little bitter about the backlash that came from his fellow owners, Giants owner John T. Brush drafted rules in January 1905 that addressed the situation going forward. The rules, which both leagues agreed to and approved, determined that the pennant-winning clubs from each respective league would face each other in the World Series. They also determined the venues and dates of the contests for the series, ticket prices and division of revenue for the teams involved, and ultimately designated the World Series as the premier event in baseball. The World Series has been contested every year since 1905

Walter Johnson (1887 - 1946), pitcher for the Washington Senators, and Philadelphia Athletics manager Connie Mack (1862 - 1956) shake hands near the dugout, 1910s.

through the 2014 season, with the lone exception being 1994 when the players' strike ended the season in mid-August.

The Giants would repeat as National League pennant winners in 1905 but would not get a crack at the Americans, who fell off the pace after their back-to-back victories. Instead, McGraw and the Giants faced another managerial legend in Connie Mack and the Philadelphia Athletics. McGraw's Giants blanked the Athletics in four of the five games to claim their first World Series championship, allowing Philadelphia just three runs in the series. While the Giants would be in the mix for the National League pennant for the remainder of the decade, they would not claim another until the 1911 season.

The majority of the rest of the decade was dominated by the Chicago teams. The White Sox claimed the 1906 American League pennant, while the Cubs were a force to be reckoned with in the National League, winning pennants in 1906, 1907, 1908 and 1910. That meant that the 1909 World Series, which featured the Detroit Tigers and Pittsburgh Pirates, was the only one that did not showcase at least one Chicago team from 1906 through 1910. These victories would prove to be the high points of both franchises as far as sustained success went.

Both teams were stockpiled with top-tier talent during this time. The White Sox boasted talent like Hall of Famers Ed Walsh and George Davis, and would add manager Hugh Duffy in 1909. The Cubs were similarly laced with Hall of Fame players during the era. Chicago was led by Mordecai "Three Finger" Brown, along with three quarters of their infield: Johnny Evers, Joe Tinker and Frank Chance. The Cubs also had Frank "Wildfire" Schulte, Harry Steinfeldt, Ed Reulbach and Orval Overall. The two teams clashed in 1906, the year that the Cubs set a major league record with 116 victories against just 36 defeats. The White Sox would get the better of things in the World Series, however, defeating the Cubs in six games.

The Cubs returned to the World Series in 1907 after racking up 107 victories, where they would face Ty Cobb and the Detroit Tigers. Led by the dominant pitching of Brown, Overall, Jack Pfiester and Reulbach, Chicago stifled the Detroit offense. After Game One ended in a 3-3 tie due to darkness, the Cubs allowed just three runs total as they swept the next four contests to claim their first World Series championship.

The two teams would clash a year later, and while Detroit's bats put some runs on the board, it wasn't enough to prevail. The Cubs rallied for five runs in the top of the ninth in Game One to win 10-6, and won the series in five games. Included in that series were shutouts in Game Four by Brown and Game Five by Overall.

The Cubs would return to the World Series in 1910, but as their veteran leaders began to age, their production went down

Duffy Lewis, outfielder for the Boston Red Sox, slides safely back to first base in the second inning of Game One of the 1916 World Series on October 7, 1916, at Fenway Park in Boston, MA.

accordingly. Despite 104 regular season wins, the Cubs couldn't overcome Chief Bender, Jack Coombs, Home Run Baker and the rest of the Philadelphia Athletics, losing the World Series in five games. Overall lasted just three innings in his one start and Reulbach was pulled after two innings in his one appearance. Brown pitched in three of the games, winning Game Four in relief, but losing Games Two and Five in which he started. The 1908 World Series victory is the most recent one for the Cubs: the 106-year span through 2014 is the longest drought between championships for any team in the four major professional sports leagues in North America.

A NORTHEASTERN FEEL: BOSTON, PHILADELPHIA DOMINATE (1910-1918)

The Athletics claimed the 1910 World Series, which came in the final year of four pennants in five years for the Cubs. It was the start of a solid run for Connie Mack's Athletics and also the Boston Red Sox. Between the two teams, they represented the American League in the World Series eight times in the nine-year span from 1910 to 1918, winning seven of those. Only the 1917 season, which saw the Chicago White Sox claim the American League pennant, kept the two teams from a clean sweep.

The Athletics were dominant at the beginning of the decade. Led by Home Run Baker, Chief Bender, Eddie Plank, Eddie Collins, Stan Coveleski, Herb Pennock and Connie Mack, the club claimed pennants in 1910, 1911, 1913 and 1914. Philadelphia won World Series titles in three of those years, claiming them in 1910, 1911 and 1913. The team beat the Cubs in five games in 1910 and followed that up with championship victories over the New York Giants in 1911 and 1913, dealing John McGraw's team defeats in six and five games, respectively. The National League representative from Boston, the Braves, swept the Athletics in the 1914 World Series.

After that surprising loss in the 1914 World Series, things went south in a hurry for the Athletics. The advent of the Federal League created further difficulties. Much like the American League did in 1901 when it declared itself a major league, the Federal League began raiding rosters of teams in both the American and National Leagues. Bender was one of many who made the transition, and over the next couple of seasons, Mack saw his stars leave. Some he traded or sold, others he released, and the loss of talent negatively impacted the franchise. They would finish last in the American League every year from 1915 to 1922.

Where Philadelphia left off, Boston picked up the pace and helped sustain the American League's dominance in the World Series. The Red Sox, who had players such as Tris Speaker, Harry Hooper, Babe Ruth and also Pennock, after the Athletics placed

The Philadelphia Athletics pose for a team photo in 1910. Connie Mack appears in street clothes, while team stars are Herb Pennock, top row, third from left, Frank Baker, second row from top, second from right, Chief Bender, second row from top, far left,Eddie Plank, third row from top, third from right, Eddie Collins, front row, far right.

him on waivers in June of 1915, were a tough team to beat in the second half of the decade. The team won pennants in 1912, 1915, 1916 and 1918, and won the World Series in each of those years. The only thing capable of hindering Boston was their ownership, which would eventually grind the team's success to a halt.

In 1912 Boston won 105 games, led by 22-year-old Smokey Joe Wood's 34-5 record and 1.91 earned-run average on the season. Speaker hit .383 with 222 hits, 10 home runs and 90 runs batted in while Duffy Lewis added a team-leading 109 runs batted in on the season. Buck O'Brien and Hugh Bedient also won 20 games each for Boston, who faced McGraw's Giants in the World Series. Just as Philadelphia dashed the hopes of McGraw and company in 1911 and 1913, the Red Sox did the same in 1912, defeating New York in seven games. Some saw it as just desserts for the Giants' refusal to play Boston in the 1904 World Series.

In 1915 all five starters in the rotation won at least 15 games: Ernie Shore and Rube Foster were both 19-8, Ruth was 18-8, Dutch Leonard was 15-7 and Wood went 15-5 for the team. Boston won 101 games and claimed the pennant by 2.5 games over the Detroit Tigers, who won 100 games of their own. Ruth hit four home runs in 92 at-bats to lead the team in that category. Boston would win the championship after beating the Phillies in five games. It was a low-scoring World Series, and Boston won the decisive fifth game, 5-4, as Harry Hooper's second home run of the game broke a 4-4 tie.

The team would repeat as the champions in 1916 after winning 91 games, which actually gave them fewer victories than the National League champion Brooklyn Robins. The Robins were 94-60 on the season but still were an underdog for the World Series. Ruth won 23 games for Boston, while Leonard and Carl Mays won 18, Shore won 16 and Rube Foster entered the rotation to pick up 14 victories. The Red Sox were dominant in the World Series, winning it in five games. Included in that was Babe Ruth's 14-inning complete-game victory in Game Two, the longest complete game in World Series history. Shore picked up two victories in the series.

Boston would finish second in 1917 to the White Sox, but they returned to win the pennant in 1918. Ruth had transitioned out of the rotation to the outfield in an effort to get his bat in the lineup more often. He hit 11 home runs and drove in 66 runs in 95 games, and also went 13-7 with a 2.22 ERA in 20 games, 19 of which were starts. Boston went 75-51 in 1918, and went on to face the Chicago Cubs in the World Series. Boston defeated the Cubs in six games to win the championship, with Ruth pitching a 1-0 shutout win over Jim "Hippo" Vaughn in Game One and

In an exciting action play, third baseman of the Philadelphia Athletics, Frank 'Home Run' Baker, dives to tag a sliding Tris Speaker, Boston Red Sox outfielder, in Boston in 1912.

then getting the win in Game Three after pitching eight innings of a 3-2 Boston victory. Mays outdueled Lefty Tyler 2-1 in the decisive sixth game to clinch the series, capping Boston's third title in four years, and fourth in seven seasons.

Things were about to change in Boston, but not in a good way. A move by Harry Frazee and its ensuing ripple effect would lead to an 86-year drought for the Red Sox between World Series championships.

1919: "THE BLACK SOX" SCANDAL AND "THE CURSE OF THE BAMBINO"

The Red Sox were riding the high of three titles in four seasons but they fell short in the 1919 season, finishing just 66-71 and in sixth place in the American League. After the season, the Red Sox and Ruth had reached an impasse that neither side was able or willing to bridge. Ruth had pitched in just 17 games that season but slammed a then-league record 29 home runs to shatter Ned Williamson's mark of 27 home runs in 1884. Ruth had been paid a salary of $10,000 in 1919 and decided that based on his performance, he deserved a raise.

Ruth demanded a raise to $20,000, which would double his salary from 1919, but owner Harry Frazee refused to meet Ruth's demands. Ruth hinted at retirement and said that he would not play for the franchise again until Frazee paid him what he felt he was worth. Frazee ran out of patience with Ruth and decided to trade him but, unfortunately for Frazee, he was limited to just two potential trade partners: the Chicago White Sox and the New York Yankees. President Ban Johnson had a strong dislike for Frazee and was attempting to remove him from ownership. That dislike led the other five teams in the American League to reject any offer from Frazee.

The White Sox offered the Red Sox Shoeless Joe Jackson and $60,000 in cash. Meanwhile, the Yankees offered a straight cash deal of $100,000, and Frazee was quick to work out a deal with them. In exchange for Ruth, Frazee received $125,000 in cash and three $25,000 notes payable each year at six percent interest. Yankee owners Jacob Ruppert and Tillinghast L'Hommedieu Huston also lent Frazee $300,000 with the collateral being the mortgage on Fenway Park. On December 26, 1919, the deal was official and Ruth was part of the Yankees. Boston won five of the first 15 World Series titles before the sale of Ruth to New York and then did not win another for 86 years.

Group portrait of baseball players of the American League's Chicago White Sox, and attorneys sitting in a courtroom in Chicago, IL.

Ruth would go on to become the premiere power hitter of the era, hammering 714 home runs before retiring in 1935. Ruth and the Yankees would win seven pennants and four World Series championships while Boston would not claim another American League pennant until 1946. Ruth led the league in

Babe Ruth is about to swing during a batting practice session before a game in 1921 at the Polo Grounds in New York City.

runs scored seven times, in home runs 10 times, and in runs batted in on six occasions during his tenure with New York. He also claimed his only American League MVP Award of his career with the Yankees, winning it in 1923.

The other major incident that took place in 1919 was not truly uncovered until the next year. The Chicago White Sox claimed the American League pennant and were heavy favorites over the Cincinnati Reds in the World Series. There was quite a bit of money wagered on the Series in favor of Cincinnati, which led to potential speculation that something suspicious was going on. The Reds prevailed in the best-of-nine series, winning it five games to three, and what happened following that tarnished the game of baseball and the reputations of some of the best players of the era.

There was no concrete evidence until September 28, 1920, when pitcher Eddie Cicotte and Shoeless Joe Jackson reportedly confessed their participation in the scheme before a grand jury in Chicago. It couldn't have come at a worse time for the White Sox, who were in a virtual tie with the Cleveland Indians for first place heading into their final series of the weekend. Owner Charles Comiskey made the correct, honorable and difficult decision to suspend Jackson, Cicotte and five other players. An eighth player who would be revealed to be the suspected ringleader, Chick Gandil, was no longer with the team.

The White Sox dropped two of their final three games to the St. Louis Browns and finished two games off the pace in the American League. Prior to the 1921 season beginning, federal judge Kenesaw Mountain Landis banned the eight players reported to be involved: Jackson, Cicotte, Gandil, Swede Risberg, Claude Williams, Happy Felsch, Buck Weaver and Fred McMullin. All eight men were banned from baseball for life, though there were several reports from the others involved that Jackson had nothing to do with the fix. Reports said that Jackson's name was mentioned to the gamblers involved in order to gain some credibility.

In the series, Jackson hit .375 (12-for-32) with five runs scored, the lone home run by either team in the series, three doubles and six runs batted in. This was in stark contrast to the .224 average that the team posted for their batting average in the series. Before the case could go to trial, key evidence went missing. This led to an acquittal of the eight individuals on August 2, 1921. A day later, however, Landis stated that he had no intention of reinstating any of the players involved. Landis's statement was as follows:

"Regardless of the verdict of juries, no player who throws a ball game, no player who undertakes or promises to throw a ball game, no player who sits in confidence with a bunch of crooked ballplayers and gamblers, where the ways and means of throwing a game are discussed and does not promptly tell his club about it, will ever play professional baseball."

The White Sox would not claim another pennant for 40 years and would not win a World Series until 86 years after the incident, with 88 years passing between titles. They had beaten the New York Giants to win the 1917 World Series, which was their last title before 2005.

THE 1920S: THE RISE OF THE YANKEES, AND THE HOUSE THAT RUTH BUILT

With Ruth a member of the Yankees beginning in the 1920 season, the American League was put on notice that the team was no longer content with being an also-ran. The team installed Ruth as an everyday player to get his bat in the lineup on a regular basis instead of just when he was pitching and he responded. He hit a robust .376 with 158 runs scored, 36 doubles, 9 triples and 137 runs batted in; he also slugged 54 home runs, nearly doubling the league record of 29 he set in his final year in Boston the season before.

The Yankees would claim the pennant six times in the 1920s, winning three in a row in 1921, 1922 and 1923, then pulling off the feat again in 1926, 1927 and 1928. The team also claimed three World Series championships in the decade, which was the most of any team during the 1920s. During this time, Ruth hit .355 with 1,365 runs scored, 1,734 hits, 314 doubles, 82 triples, 467 home runs and 1,331 runs batted in. To say that he was worth every penny that the team paid for him in 1919 would be a vast understatement.

The Yankees were not the only team to claim multiple championships in the decade, however. They weren't even the only team from their city to earn more than one World Series title in the 1920s: the New York Giants, still led by John McGraw, won back-to-back titles in 1921 and 1922, both at the expense of the Yankees. The Giants claimed four straight National League pennants from 1921 through 1924 to lead the NL in that category.

The Washington Senators were the only other American League team to win multiple pennants in the decade, winning back-to-back flags in 1924 and 1925. Cleveland (1920) and Philadelphia (1929) also won a pennant each. Meanwhile, in the National League, besides the Giants' four pennants, St. Louis and Pittsburgh won a pair of pennants each, while Brooklyn (1920) and the Cubs (1929) claimed the remaining ones. The

Babe Ruth, New York Yankees outfielder, right, talks about the finer points of hitting with teammate and first baseman Lou Gehrig in June 1923.

Indians won the World Series in 1920, followed by the Giants in 1921 and 1922; the Yankees in 1923, 1927 and 1928; the Washington Senators in 1924; the Pittsburgh Pirates in 1925; the St. Louis Cardinals in 1926; and the Philadelphia Athletics in 1929 to close out the decade.

There were several terrific individual accomplishments during the decade as well. Rogers Hornsby won a total of seven National League batting titles, including six in a row for the St. Louis Cardinals. His seventh batting title came with the Boston Braves in 1928. In the American League, Harry Heilman of the Detroit Tigers won four batting titles to lead the way. George Sisler of the St. Louis Browns was the only other player with multiple batting titles, with two.

THE 1930S: A NEW YORK STATE OF MIND, RUTH RETIRES, DIMAGGIO DEBUTS

The New York Yankees picked up in the 1930s where they left off in the 1920s. The team had Ruth, Lou Gehrig, Tony Lazzeri, Bill Dickey and company in the lineup, and Lefty Gomez and Red Ruffing headlining the rotation. After six pennants and three World Series championships in the 1920s, the Yankees followed that up with five more pennants in the 1930s and won World Series championships in each of those seasons. New York won four straight World Series championships from 1936 through 1939.

The Giants claimed a World Series as well, winning in 1933 over the Senators, and also claimed National League pennants in 1936 and 1937. The problem for the Giants in those years was that their opponent was the powerhouse Yankees. The Cardinals were the only National League team to claim multiple championships in the 1930s, winning in both 1931 and 1934 after being defeated in the 1930 World Series by the Philadelphia Athletics. The Detroit Tigers' championship in 1935 made them the only American League team other than the Yankees to win a title during the decade.

New York Yankee Joe DiMaggio (1914 - 1999) with his teammates in the dugout at the Yankee Training Camp in St. Petersburg, FL.

The 1930s also brought about the end of several prolific careers and the start of two very prominent, intertwined ones. Babe Ruth retired after playing his final game on May 30, 1935. He was signed by the Boston Braves after the Yankees decided to part ways with the aging slugger but played in just 28 games with the Braves, hitting six home runs but posting just a .181 batting average, before hanging up his cleats. Later in the decade, Ruth's teammate Lou Gehrig hung his up as well. Gehrig's final game was April 30, 1939. He had played in a then-record 2,130 consecutive games and was a force to be reckoned with in the Yankees lineup. Gehrig would die just over two years later, a victim of amyotrophic lateral sclerosis (ALS), or what is now called Lou Gehrig's disease.

While Gehrig and Ruth were leaving the sport, future stars Joe DiMaggio of the Yankees and Ted Williams of the Boston Red Sox were among those who were just breaking in and making a name for themselves in the big leagues. DiMaggio began his career after being acquired from the San Francisco Seals and made his pro debut in 1936. He would play for the Yankees through 1951, missing the 1943-1945 seasons due to World War II. Williams made his debut for the Red Sox in 1939, and played for the club through 1960. Williams had two stints in the military which interrupted his time with Boston: he missed 1943-1945 as did DiMaggio, but also played in just six games in 1952 and 37 in 1953. Williams was recalled from a list of inactive reserves to be part of the Korean War effort.

THE 1940S: YANKEES AND CARDINALS RULE, DIMAGGIO'S 56 AND WILLIAMS' .406

The 1940s were again primarily dominated by the Yankees, a trend that would continue through the 1950s as well. New York claimed five American League pennants (1941, 1942, 1943, 1947 and 1949) along with four World Series championships (1941, 1943, 1947 and 1949). Three of the Yankees' World Series victories came over the Brooklyn Dodgers; those two teams would clash on several more occasions over the coming decades.

While the Yankees were dominating the American League, the St. Louis Cardinals were the elite that the National League had to offer. The Cardinals claimed four National League pennants (1942, 1943, 1944, and 1946) and three World Series championships (1942, 1944 and 1946). The Dodgers claimed National League pennants in 1941, 1947 and 1949, but had the unfortunate circumstance of playing the Yankees in each of those series, thus coming up empty handed in regard to championships. With St. Louis and Brooklyn combining for seven of the ten pennants in the decade, there wasn't much left for anyone else. Cincinnati (1940), the Cubs (1945) and the Boston Braves (1948) were the only others to win National League pennants. Only the Reds captured a World Series championship, defeating the Detroit Tigers in seven games. In the American League, the Tigers were the only other team with multiple pennants, winning them in 1940 and 1945. The St. Louis Browns (1944), Boston Red Sox

Jackie Robinson, first baseman for the Brooklyn Dodgers, leaps for a throw during warm ups before a game in 1947 at Ebbets Field.

(1947) and Cleveland Indians (1948) won the other American League pennants in the decade. Detroit was victorious in 1945, while the Indians defeated the Braves in 1948 to win the World Series. To date, it is the last World Series championship that the Indians franchise has to their credit: the team was defeated in 1954, 1995 and 1997.

The decade's significance extends beyond pennant winners and championship victories, however. On April 15, 1947, Jackie Robinson of the Brooklyn Dodgers broke the color barrier and became the first black player in Major League Baseball since the 1880s. Robinson would play with the team for a decade, winning the inaugural Rookie of the Year Award in 1947. Dodgers manager Leo Durocher quickly quashed a potential mutiny of players that didn't want to play with Robinson, and things went smoothly within the organization after that incident.

The 1940s also saw the epic duel between Ted Williams and Joe DiMaggio in 1941. The Yankees would claim the pennant that year while the Red Sox were a distant second, but the difference in the standings had little bearing on what the two men did on the field. DiMaggio started a hitting streak on May 15, with a 1-for-4 performance off Eddie Smith of the Chicago White Sox. The trend would continue, as DiMaggio kept picking up at least one hit per game over the next several weeks.

Heading into a doubleheader against the Washington Senators on June 29, DiMaggio had hit in 40 straight games, one game shy of George Sisler's modern-day record of 41 consecutive games with a hit. DiMaggio doubled in the first game to tie the mark and then singled in the second game to surpass Sisler with a 42-game run. Two days later, back at Yankee Stadium, a crowd of 52,832 fans saw DiMaggio single, which tied Wee Willie Keeler's 44-game hitting streak, the longest in baseball history. The next day, DiMaggio homered against Williams and the Red Sox, breaking the mark and extending his streak to 45 games. He would eventually extend his streak to 56 games before a 0-for-4 performance against the Cleveland Indians on July 17. Third baseman Ken Keltner made two tremendous plays to rob DiMaggio of potential hits, but DiMaggio promptly got a hit the next day and would hit in 17 consecutive games, giving him hits in 73 of 74 contests.

While DiMaggio was running up his hitting streak, Ted Williams was working on being consistent throughout the course of the season. Williams had his average up to as high as .430 in late May and was still hitting at a .413 clip in mid- September before his average began to decline. On September 28, the final day of the season, Williams was hitting .39955, which would round up to a .400 average if he did not play or have an official at-bat on the afternoon. The last player to hit .400 in the major leagues prior to 1941 was Bill Terry of the New York Giants in 1930.

When presented with the option of sitting out a doubleheader against the Philadelphia Athletics, Williams decided to play. His rationale was that if he couldn't hit .400 by playing, he didn't deserve that average. Williams proceeded to go 4-for-5 in the opening game and 2-for-3 in the nightcap. The 6-for-8 performance boosted his average to .406 on the season, and he would finish the season with 37 home runs and 120 runs batted in, while the .406 average gave him the first of his six batting titles. In the end, DiMaggio would win the American League MVP Award, while Williams would finish second.

Larry Doby, outfielder for the Cleveland Indians, is congratulated by teammate and manager Lou Boudreau at Fenway Park's home plate after hitting a home run on May 10, 1948.

THE 1950S: YANKEE PRIDE, LARSEN'S PERFECT GAME AND WESTWARD RELOCATION

The 1950s were more of the same thing, different decade: the Yankees continued to dominate the American League, and all of baseball for that matter. New York claimed an astonishing eight American League pennants and picked up another six World Series championships, including four in a row from 1950 through 1953. New York also won the World Series in 1956 and 1958, and came up on the short end in 1955 and 1957, giving them two sets of four consecutive pennants in the decade. The only other teams to get in the action in the American League were the Indians in 1954 and the White Sox in 1959. The Indians were swept by Willie Mays and the Giants, while the White Sox were defeated by the Dodgers in six games.

The Dodgers won five National League pennants in the decade: 1952, 1953, 1955, 1956 and 1959. The team also captured two World Series crowns, coming up victorious in 1955 and 1959, the former against the Yankees, their heated rival. The Yankees earned three of their six championships in the decade at the Dodgers' expense however. The New York Giants (1951, 1954) and the Milwaukee Braves (1957, 1958), along with the Philadelphia Phillies (1950), rounded out the National League champions. The Dodgers' collapse in 1951, which allowed the Giants to rally from a 13.5-game deficit in August to force a three-game playoff, was a disappointment for Brooklyn fans.

While Brooklyn snapped the Yankees' hex over them with a victory in the 1955 World Series, they would find themselves victimized by something that, through the 2014 World Series, has not been seen again. In Game Five of the 1956 World Series, Don Larsen, who would finish his career with a record of 81-91, would accomplish a feat as rare as any in Major League Baseball. On that crisp October day in the Bronx, Larsen faced 27 hitters and retired every one of them. Not one Brooklyn hitter reached base via hit, walk, error or any other way—it is the only perfect

Mickey Mantle takes a mighty swing at a pitch during a road game in June 1958. Mantle would go on to lead the Yankees to capturing the 1958 World Series championship against the Milwaukee Braves.

game in World Series history, or in playoff history for that matter. There have been only 20 perfect games thrown in the history of baseball through 2014. The Yankees would go on to win the 1956 World Series in seven games. Larsen outdueled Sal Maglie of Brooklyn, who gave up just two runs on five hits in the defeat.

The 1950s also brought about several franchise relocations: the Braves moved from Boston to Milwaukee in time for the 1953 season; the St. Louis Browns moved to Baltimore in 1954 and became the Baltimore Orioles; and the Philadelphia Athletics uprooted their franchise and relocated to Kansas City. While these moves were all surprising, the two that would come following the 1957 season changed the sport dramatically.

Prior to 1957, there were no teams further west than the Midwestern United States. That changed quickly when the Brooklyn Dodgers, under owner Walter O'Malley, made the decision to relocate their franchise across the country to Los Angeles. In order to get the league to sign off on that move, O'Malley had to convince another team to move to the West Coast with him. O'Malley worked on New York Giants majority owner Horace Stoneham about the prospect of moving and, at the same time, San Francisco mayor George Christopher was making overtures toward the Giants ownership as well. In the summer of 1957, a deal was struck and the Giants made the announcement that they, too, were moving to California and would play in San Francisco. Beginning in 1958, the Yankees were the only team left in New York, and it would remain that way until 1962 when expansion brought the New York Mets.

Roger Maris (1934 - 1985) of the New York Yankees leans into a pitch and hits his 60th home run of the season, tying Babe Ruth's record, New York, NY.

THE 1960S: MARIS BREAKS RUTH'S MARK, EXPANSION AND DIVISIONAL PLAY BEGIN

The 1960s continued to further the change in baseball's landscape that the 1950s began. With the changes in location, including the placement of teams on the West Coast, the game was more prevalent across the entire country instead of just east of the Mississippi River. Baseball had some decisions to make about the viability of having just two teams out on the West Coast, and how that would impact travel, among other issues. The decision that was made would again revamp the sport.

The league opted to expand, and added four new teams, two each in 1961 and 1962. The two teams added in 1961 were the Los Angeles Angels and the Washington Senators. The Senators were added to replace the previous incarnation of the franchise, which moved to Minnesota following the 1960 season and became the Twins. Both clubs were added to the American League, giving it 10 teams in 1961 while the National League still featured eight. The leagues were quickly evened out with the addition of the Houston Colt .45s and the New York Mets to the National League in 1962. Of the four teams, only the Mets have kept the same name throughout their franchise's history.

Expansion drafts were held so the teams could stock their rosters with players. Each draft was league-specific: when the Angels and Senators drafted in 1961, they chose from American League players, and when the Mets and Colt .45s chose in 1962, the pool of available players was comprised of those who were on National League rosters. None of the four teams were successful in their first season. The Angels were 70-91, the Colt .45s went 64-96, Washington was 61-100, and the Mets were 40-120, the worst record in baseball history since the 162-game schedule was adopted. The Colt .45s and Mets were so bad that the National League had a second, smaller expansion draft in 1963 to try to help the teams.

While the 1961 expansion did create a buzz due to there being more teams to follow, it also threatened to water down the talent pool. The season was big for reasons other than expansion, however. The schedule was lengthened from 154 to 162 games, and it led to a pronounced threat on Babe Ruth's single-season home run record. Ruth had slammed 60 home runs in 1927, a record that had not truly been threatened since. When Mickey Mantle chased it and fell short, hitting 52 in 1956, the media was rooting against Mantle.

The 1961 season saw Mantle and his Yankee teammate, Roger Maris, chase after Ruth's record. The two men were hitting home runs at a prodigious rate, as was the rest of Major League Baseball. This prompted commissioner Ford C. Frick to declare that if the record was broken after the 154th game of the season (the number of games played in 1927), there would be a note in the record book stating that it took place in a 162-game season. While Mantle slowed down and would finish the season with 54 home runs, Maris kept slugging right along. The 154th game came and passed with Maris at 59 home runs. He would hit his 60th to tie Ruth in game 159 of the season. Jack Fisher of the Baltimore Orioles gave up that home run. On October 1 in the final game of the season, Maris homered off Tracy Stallard of the Red Sox, giving him 61 home runs and the record.

The first half of the 1960s was the end of an era for the Yankees. They claimed the first five pennants of the decade, winning two World Series, and then wouldn't win another pennant until 1976. Age and the retirement of key players finally

Jim Gilliam #19 of the Los Angeles Dodgers in action against the New York Mets during an Major League Baseball game circa 1962 at the Polo Grounds in the Manhattan borough of New York City, NY.

caught up with the team, and they were unable to replace the pieces as easily and effectively as they once were. That led to other teams making their presence known. The Twins claimed the 1965 pennant, while Baltimore won the American League flag in 1966 and 1969. Boston won the pennant in 1967, and Detroit took the honors in 1968. The Orioles won the World Series in 1966, while Detroit came through in 1968.

The decade was also marked by further expansion and the advent of divisional play in 1969. That year, baseball expanded by four teams, and realigned both the American and National Leagues from a 10-team free-for-all into two six-team divisions per league. The Seattle Pilots, Kansas City Royals, Montreal Expos and San Diego Padres all joined in 1969, with one team going to each of the new divisions. The Mets rallied in the final two months of the season to claim the National League pennant, and then defeated the heavily favored Orioles to win the first World Series in franchise history, and the first World Series contested in the divisional play era.

The decade wouldn't have been complete without a few other happenings. The Braves relocated again, this time from Milwaukee to Atlanta, in 1966. Charlie Finley moved the Athletics from Kansas City to Oakland in 1967. Carl Yastrzemski won the American League Triple Crown in 1967, a year after Baltimore's Frank Robinson. Another wouldn't be won until 2012, when Miguel Cabrera accomplished the feat.

Meanwhile, the 1968 season was the "Year of the Pitcher" as team batting averages plummeted and pitchers racked up eye-popping numbers. Bob Gibson of the Cardinals posted a modern-era record 1.12 ERA on the season. Luis Tiant led the American League with a 1.60 ERA and allowed opposing hitters to hit just .168 against him, another major league record. Denny McLain of the Detroit Tigers became the first pitcher since Dizzy Dean in 1934 to win at least 30 games in a season, as he won 31. In 1,625 regular season contests between both leagues, 339 of them ended in a shutout victory. The Cardinals had 30 of them on their own. Following the season, expansion and the changing of the strike zone back to what it was before the 1963 season brought numbers back to some form of normalcy.

Jim Spencer of the New York Yankees pours champagne on team owner George Steinbrenner as they celebrate winning the 1978 World Series over the Los Angeles Dodgers on October 17, 1978, at Dodger Stadium in Los Angeles, CA.

THE 1970S: ALL-STAR DRAMA, THE BIG RED MACHINE AND A WEST COAST THREEPEAT

The 1970s were an abnormal decade compared to the previous five decades in Major League Baseball. This can mainly be attributed to the fact that the Yankees were no longer the dominant team in the sport, or in the American League for that matter. The team did claim three straight pennants from 1976 to 1978 and won championships in 1977 and 1978, but those numbers pale in comparison to the statistics that the franchise racked up since the deal to acquire Babe Ruth in December of 1919.

Change came to the Yankees in 1973, when George Steinbrenner bought the franchise for $8.8 million. "The Boss," as Steinbrenner was known, was a fixture for the franchise over the next few decades. He was famous for hiring and firing managers, and signing high-profile, and often high-priced, players. Steinbrenner would be a major presence, if not a titan, in the world of professional sports, much to the dismay—and often chagrin—of fellow owners.

Perhaps one of the most famous moments in the decade happened early on, coming in the 1970 season. On July 14, 1970, at the newly opened Riverfront Stadium in Cincinnati, the National League and American League All-Star teams did battle in the All-Star Game. Most All-Star Games are about fun and entertaining the fans as opposed to serious competition. This one would deviate from that plan, mainly due to the presence of Charlie Hustle himself, Pete Rose.

Things got competitive after the National League rallied for three runs in the bottom of the ninth inning to tie the game at four and send it to extra innings. American League pitcher Clyde Wright got the first two outs in the bottom of the 12th inning. Rose singled to keep the inning alive and took second following a single by Billy Grabarkewitz. That brought Jim Hickman of the Chicago Cubs to the plate, and he promptly delivered a base hit to center field. Amos Otis fielded the ball cleanly and fired a perfect throw to the plate with plenty of time to cut down Rose. Cleveland's Ray Fosse caught the ball and prepared to tag Rose out and send the game to the 13th inning.

But Rose didn't slow down or go into a slide. He barreled in on Fosse and ran into him at full speed. The collision injured both players and stunned Fosse enough that he dropped the ball. Rose was safe and the National League had a 5-4 victory, their eighth consecutive win in the Midsummer Classic. Fosse ended up with a fractured and dislocated shoulder in the collision, though the damage was not determined immediately. He played for a month after the injury was sustained and never reached the numbers he had prior to the injury.

The Reds and Rose, along with catcher Johnny Bench, second baseman Joe Morgan and a strong cast of supporting members, formed a dynamo known as the "Big Red Machine." While the Reds made the World Series in 1970 and 1972 before being defeated, it was not until the 1975 season that all the

Outfielder Reggie Jackson of the Oakland Athletics.

pieces were in place for a serious run at the title. Cincinnati won back-to-back World Series titles in 1976, defeating the Boston Red Sox in seven hard-fought games before sweeping the Yankees a year later.

The series with Boston was a back-and-forth affair. Leading three games to two, the Reds had a 6-3 lead in the eighth inning of Game Six at Fenway Park. Pedro Borbon gave up a single to Fred Lynn to lead off the inning and followed that with a walk to Rico Petrocelli. Sparky Anderson made the move to bring in Rawly Eastwick, who struck out Dwight Evans and retired Rick Burleson on a lineout to record the second out of the inning. The Red Sox went with pinch-hitter Bernie Carbo to hit for Roger Moret. On a 2-2 pitch, one pitch after an awkward swing to foul a pitch off, Carbo slugged a three-run home run to knot the score at six and send the game to extra innings.

Boston blew a prime chance to win the game in the ninth, loading the bases with no outs, but Denny Doyle was cut down at the plate after Fred Lynn hit a short fly ball to left to end the threat. Cincinnati nearly won the game in the 11th when Dwight Evans robbed Morgan on a drive to left field, and then had the presence of mind to double off Ken Griffey Sr. at first base to end the inning. Cincinnati had back-to-back singles with one out in the 12th, but came up empty as well.

In the bottom of the frame, with the eighth Cincinnati pitcher of the game starting his third inning of work, catcher Carlton Fisk lofted the second pitch of the inning down the left-field line. Fisk was waving as he went down the first base line, seemingly trying to keep the ball fair. As it turned out, Fisk's drive slammed off the foul pole just above the Green Monster in left field for a walk-off home run. Boston won the game, 7-6, in 12 innings to tie the series. They had no magic left for Game Seven, however: Boston blew a 3-0 lead, giving up the winning run in the top of the ninth to lose the game and the series, 4-3, and extending their drought without a championship to 57 years.

Pete Rose of the Philadelphia Phillies.

While Boston struggled, a new dynasty popped onto the radar screen in the early 1970s. The Oakland Athletics, who had moved to the city in 1968, made a major impact on baseball, claiming back-to-back-to-back World Series titles in 1972, 1973, and 1974. The team also made the American League Championship Series in 1971 and 1975 before being defeated. Led by stars such as Reggie Jackson, Catfish Hunter, Vida Blue, Ken Holtzman and Rollie Fingers, the Athletics dominated the American League Western Division for the first half of the decade before faltering. The Athletics are the only team in major league history besides the Yankees to win three consecutive World Series championships.

Two teams were added to the American League in 1977. The Seattle Mariners and Toronto Blue Jays were the sport's first additions since the 1969 advent of divisional play. The Seattle franchise replaced the Seattle Pilots, who moved to Milwaukee after their inaugural season of 1969 and became the Brewers. The Blue Jays joined the Montreal Expos as teams that played outside the United States.

THE 1980S: THE PLAYERS STRIKE, PARITY AND THE START OF "THE STREAK"

Baseball in the 1980s was markedly different from what fans had seen in previous decades. Instead of a dominant team, parity broke out across the league: nine different teams claimed World Series victories in the decade, with only the Los Angeles Dodgers claiming multiple championships (1981, 1988). Milwaukee, Kansas City and San Diego made their World Series debuts. All three teams came up on the short end of the stick in their debut, though the Royals would return to claim the 1985 World Series championship in seven games over St. Louis.

The 1981 season was marred by the fifth work stoppage since 1972, and this one was by far the most costly of the lot up to that point. While the 1972 strike cost baseball two weeks' worth of games and the stoppages in 1973, 1976 and 1980 were resolved in spring training, the 1981 version was ugly. It lasted 50 days, from June 12 through July 31, wiping out 712 games from the slate, and it forced baseball to split its season into two halves, with the champion in each division in the first half playing the champion of the second half in a best-of-five series. Attendance dropped in 17 of baseball's 24 cities after the strike, and television ratings suffered accordingly.

Baltimore Orioles third baseman Cal Ripken (C) falls on top of Toronto Blue Jays base runner Shawn Green after Green hit a triple in the seventh inning in Baltimore 29 June. Toronto went on to beat the Orioles, 3-2, and sweep the four game series.

This was the first decade since the acquisition of Babe Ruth that the Yankees failed to win multiple American League pennants. It also was the first time since Ruth joined the team that New York failed to win a World Series championship, as they were defeated by the Dodgers in their lone appearance in 1981. In the American League, only Kansas City (1980, 1985) and Oakland (1988, 1989) won multiple pennants, while in the National League, St. Louis won three pennants (1982, 1985,

Pitcher Dave Stieb of the Toronto Blue Jays pitches against the Seattle Mariners during a MLB game on May 12, 1985, in Toronto, ON.

1987) and the Dodgers (1981, 1988) and Phillies (1980, 1983) each won a pair of National League flags.

The 1980s also brought some interesting statistics to light. The Minnesota Twins won just 85 games in the regular season in 1987, the fewest victories for a World Series champion to that point in time. The Twins also had dismal home/road splits. While they were a stellar 56-25 at the Metrodome, the team was a dreadful 29-52 on the road. They ended up with home-field advantage in the World Series in 1987 against the Cardinals, and it proved crucial; Minnesota was 0-3 in St. Louis at Busch Stadium but won all four games at the Metrodome, giving them the World Series title. It marked the first time in World Series history that all seven games were won by the home team.

Cal Ripken Jr.'s ironman streak began in the 1980s as well. Ripken started his streak on May 30, 1982, and would not miss another game for the Orioles until September 20, 1998. In that 16-plus year span, Ripken played in a record 2,632 consecutive games. Other firsts and interesting feats in the decade included Milwaukee's Juan Nieves throwing a no-hitter on April 15, 1987. Nieves was the first Brewer and first Puerto Rican-born major league pitcher to throw a no-hitter in the majors. Additionally, there was Bill Buckner's miscue in Game Six of the 1986 World Series, which sunk Boston, and Leon Durham's fateful error in Game Five of the 1984 National League Championship Series, which cost the Cubs against the San Diego Padres.

Roger Clemens became the first pitcher to strike out 20 hitters in a nine-inning game on April 29, 1986, for the Red Sox. Pete Rose became baseball's all-time hit king with his 4,192nd career hit, a single off San Diego's Eric Show on September 11, 1985. Orel Hershisher set a major league record by throwing 59 consecutive scoreless innings for the Dodgers in 1988, breaking former Dodger Don Drysdale's record. Sticking with the Dodgers, Kirk Gibson's pinch-hit, two-run home run in Game One of the World Series off Oakland closer Dennis Eckersley provided one of the most dramatic moments in baseball history.

THE 1990S: STRIKE CANCELS WORLD SERIES, MORE EXPANSION, AND THE HOME RUN CHASE

The 1990s were a time of change and intrigue in Major League Baseball. The league saw its first expansion in 16 years when the Colorado Rockies and Florida Marlins were added to the National League in 1993. Baseball would further expand by two more teams in 1998, adding the Arizona Diamondbacks in the National League and the Tampa Bay Devil Rays (later shortened to Rays) in the American League. Baseball also realigned from two divisions per league to three in 1994.

The 1994 season was a black mark on professional baseball. Unable to reach an agreement with the owners, the players walked off the job on August 12, 1994. One of the major sticking points at the time was the owners' desire to implement a salary cap. The players, who could have gone on strike in September 1993, set that August 12 date in late July 1994. Ownership would not agree to a deal, which included a proposal by the union where the 16 highest payroll teams would be taxed, with that money going to the 12 remaining clubs in a form of revenue sharing. Also included in that proposal was that teams would share 25 percent of all gate receipts. Ownership claimed that the costs for teams would not be met, and the proposal was rejected.

In the end, baseball never resumed play in 1994 and acting commissioner Bud Selig cancelled the remainder of the season, including the World Series, on September 14, 1994. It marked the first time that the World Series was not played since the infamous snub by John McGraw and the Giants 90 years earlier. The strike ruined things for the Montreal Expos, who were 74-40 that season, the best record in all of Major League Baseball. The strike also came at an inopportune time for San Diego's Tony Gwynn, who was hitting .394 in his efforts to become the first player since Ted Williams in 1941 to hit .400 in a season, and for San Francisco's Matt Williams, who smacked 43 home runs for the Giants, who still had 47 games to play in the season. He was on pace to challenge Roger Maris's home run mark of 61.

Baseball would not return to normalcy until April 2, 1995, 232 days after the strike officially began.

As it would turn out, Maris's record would be broken, just not in 1994. It would happen in 1998, with St. Louis Cardinals first baseman Mark McGwire and Chicago Cubs right fielder Sammy Sosa putting on the power hitting display. McGwire hit 16 home runs in May and had 27 by the end of that month. Meanwhile, Sosa, who had just 13 home runs the first two months, set a new major league record when he slammed 20 home runs during the month of June. By the end of August, Sosa and McGwire had both smacked 55 home runs, leaving them on pace to shatter Maris's record.

Moises Alou #18 of the Montreal Expos scores during a MLB game against the Atlanta Braves on July 25, 1994, in Atlanta, GA.

Sammy Sosa #21 of the Chicago Cubs bats during a Major League Baseball game circa 1992 at Wrigley Field in Chicago, IL. Sosa played for the Cubs 1992-2004.

Oddly enough, McGwire was at 60 home runs entering a series with the Cubs in early September. On September 7 McGwire homered off Mike Morgan for his 61st home run, joining Maris as the only two men to that point to reach the number. The next night, McGwire hit his record-breaking 62nd home run off Steve Trachsel to establish a new record. Sosa would catch up to McGwire when he hit his 62nd against the Milwaukee Brewers. Entering the final series of the season for both teams, both McGwire and Sosa had 65 home runs apiece. Sosa homered off Jose Lima of the Astros to give him the lead briefly with his 66th home run, but he would not hit another for the rest of the season. McGwire homered five times off of five different Montreal pitchers to finish with 70. Sosa would claim the National League MVP Award for his efforts, as the Cubs clinched the wild card with a one-game playoff victory over the San Francisco Giants.

In the postseason, the Blue Jays became the first team not from the United States to win the World Series, claiming their first championship in 1992. For good measure, the team repeated as champions in 1993. The Yankees returned to form, winning three championships: they defeated the Atlanta Braves in 1996 and 1999, and knocked off the San Diego Padres in 1998. The expansion Florida Marlins, in just their fifth season of existence, became the first wild-card team to win a World Series title when they defeated the Cleveland Indians in seven games during the 1997 World Series. The Braves made the postseason every year from 1991 through 1999, but won just one World Series championship in 1995.

THE 2000S TO TODAY: BONDS BREAKS MCGWIRE, AARON'S MARKS, END OF TWO CHAMPIONSHIP DROUGHTS, BARTMAN'S BLUNDER

Since the turn of the century, Major League Baseball has not disappointed the fans in terms of exciting contests, record-breaking performances and moments that will not soon be forgotten. While the San Francisco Giants have claimed three titles and both the Yankees and the St. Louis Cardinals have won two championships each during this time, more surprising clubs have made their way to becoming World Series champions as well. A mix of traditional powers and newer contenders has made for an interesting baseball landscape.

The Boston Red Sox entered the new millennium with an old problem: the inability to win a World Series championship. The team's last title entering the year 2000 was 1918, back when Babe Ruth was still playing for them. The championship drought was a fact that was rarely overlooked by the media. Yankees fans, who love to torment Bostonians with their successes and the Red Sox' futilities, also made it a point to drive the fact home at any possible opportunity.

That all changed in 2004. The Yankees had their foot firmly on the Red Sox' throats, leading Boston three games to none in the AL Championship Series, and were up by a run in the ninth inning of Game Four with Mariano Rivera on the mound. Dave Roberts stole second base and scored on a single by Bill Mueller to tie the game. David Ortiz's 12th-inning home run off of Paul Quantrill gave Boston a 6-4 win and a bit of life in the series.

The Yankees were poised to wipe out Boston in Game Five, leading 4-2 in the eighth inning. The game went to extra innings and Boston prevailed, 5-4, on Ortiz's game-winning single in the bottom of the 14th inning. Curt Schilling pitched seven gutty innings in Game Six with a bloody sock and Mark Bellhorn's three-run homer proved to be the difference in a 4-2 Boston win.

For all the drama that Games Four, Five and Six brought, Seven was a disappointment, especially for New York fans. Boston jumped out to a 6-0 lead after two innings, highlighted by Johnny Damon's grand slam off Javier Vazquez, en route to a 10-3 win and the AL pennant. Boston went on to sweep the Cardinals to win their first World Series in 86 years. For good measure, the Red Sox added championships in 2007, when they

The Boston Red Sox celebrate after teammate David Ortiz #34 hit the game-winning homerun to defeat the Anaheim Angels 8-6 in the 10th inning of Game Three of the American League Division Series on October 8, 2004, at Fenway Park in Boston, MA. The Red Sox swept the best-of-five series.

swept the Colorado Rockies, who had staged an improbable rally in September to make the postseason as a wild card, and in 2013 when the Red Sox knocked off the Cardinals in six games.

The Chicago White Sox also ended their 88-year drought without a championship. In 2005 the team from the south side of Chicago swept the Houston Astros, who had made their first trip to the World Series. It had been 46 years since the White Sox had even appeared in a World Series, with their last showing being a loss in 1959 to the Los Angeles Dodgers.

While Boston and the White Sox put their demons to bed, the Chicago Cubs found a new way to be plagued by one. In 2003, after leading the Florida Marlins three games to one in the NL Championship Series and holding a 3-0 lead in the top of the eighth inning of Game Six at Wrigley Field, disaster struck the Cubs. On a foul ball hit by Luis Castillo down the left field line, a fan reached for the ball and deflected it away from left fielder Moises Alou. Castillo later worked a walk out of the at-bat. Alex Gonzalez booted a double-play grounder later in the inning, and the Marlins scored eight runs in the frame, forcing a decisive Game Seven. Florida took Game Seven and beat the Yankees in six games to claim their second championship.

A look at the decade-plus that has gone by in the new millennium would be incomplete without discussing one Barry Lamar Bonds. In 2001 Bonds broke the single-season home run mark set in 1998 by Mark McGwire. Bonds hit his 71st home run of the season off Chan Ho Park of the Los Angeles Dodgers on October 5. He added his 72nd off Park in the same game before hitting his 73rd home run of the year off Dennis Springer on October 7. Bonds won four straight NL MVP Awards between 2001 and 2004. He hit 209 home runs in that span.

Bonds tied Babe Ruth's mark of 714 career home runs on May 14, 2006, with a shot off Oakland's Brad Halsey in an interleague game. On May 28 Bonds surpassed Ruth with his 715th career home run, this coming off Colorado's Byung-Hung Kim. On August 4, 2007, Bonds tied the great Hank Aaron's

Fans interfere with outfielder Moises Alou #18 of the Chicago Cubs on a ball hit by Luis Castillo #1 of the Florida Marlins in the eighth inning during Game Six of the National League Championship Series October 14, 2003, at Wrigley Field in Chicago, IL.

mark of 755 career home runs with a blast off San Diego reliever Clay Hensley. Three nights later, on August 7, 2007, Bonds surpassed Aaron, hitting his 756th career home run off Washington's Mike Bacsik to break the mark. He finished the season with 28 home runs to end up with 762 in his career and then retired.

There is plenty of controversy as to whether Bonds used performance-enhancing drugs in the latter stages of his career. He congratulated Mark McGwire when McGwire admitted to using steroids, but declined to speak about himself. Bonds was indicted on perjury and obstruction of justice charges relating to the BALCO scandal in 2007 but after all four defendants, including Bonds' trainer, Greg Anderson, took pleas in court that allowed them to not reveal names of players who used steroids, there has been no concrete evidence one way or the other.

The Philadelphia Phillies won their first championship since 1980 by defeating the Tampa Bay Rays, who won their first AL pennant, in the 2008 World Series. Philadelphia repeated as NL champs in 2009 but fell in six games to the Yankees. They are the last team in the NL to win back-to-back pennants. The last team in the AL to repeat as pennant winners was the Texas Rangers, who claimed the AL flag in both 2010 and 2011 only to fall short in the World Series each time. The Giants defeated the Rangers in five games in 2010 while the Cardinals beat Texas in seven games in 2011.

Pitching has seemingly improved in recent years as the power numbers that ran rampant in the first part of the new millennium have dropped precipitously. Between 2000 and 2009, there were 12 instances where a player hit at least 50 home runs in a season. From 2010 to 2014, there have been two: Jose Bautista hit 54 home runs in 2010 and Chris Davis hit 53 in 2013. The home run leader in 2014 was Nelson Cruz, who hit 40.

That 2010 title was the first of three in the last five years for the Giants, who have claimed World Series crowns in 2010, 2012 and 2014. San Francisco swept the Detroit Tigers in the 2012 World Series and had to go seven games to defeat the Kansas City Royals in the 2014 World Series. Madison Bumgarner put together a terrific postseason performance for the Giants in 2014, especially in the World Series, as he went 2-0 with a save. He pitched five innings to close out Game Seven as the Giants won 3-2 and took the championship.

The 2014 season was the end of Bud Selig's run as commissioner of Major League Baseball. After assuming the role of acting commissioner in 1992, he officially took over in 1998. Under Selig's watch the World Baseball Classic was created, the league continually set new attendance marks, interleague play and the wild card were introduced, and revenues increased by nearly 400 percent. Selig saw MLB through the 1994 strike that led to the cancellation of the World Series that year and the shortening of the 1995 season.

Barry Bonds of the San Francisco Giants acknowledges the crowd after hitting career home run number 715 to pass Babe Ruth on the all time list during the game against the Colorado Rockies at AT&T Park in San Francisco, CA on May 28, 2006. The Rockies defeated the Giants 6-3.

Selig was on the job when the most recent expansion took place, when the Tampa Bay Rays and Arizona Diamondbacks joined the league. He moved the Brewers from the AL to the NL and later moved the Astros from the NL to the AL, realigned the league from four divisions to six, awarded home-field advantage in the World Series to the league that won the All-Star Game, added a second wild-card team to each league and came up with the use of expanded instant replay to help ensure that controversial calls were correct.

Selig will always be remembered as being part of the issue regarding the rampant use of PEDs and steroids in the late 1990s and early 2000s. The Mitchell Report determined that in addition to the teams and players, he was also responsible for the problems that plagued baseball during that time. The report and the issues that took place were major reasons for the implementation of a stricter policy on PEDs. With Selig's retirement, chief operating officer of Major League Baseball Rob Manfred Jr. assumed the role of commissioner on January 25, 2015, after being elected to the post on August 14, 2014.

ABOVE: *MLB Commissioner Bud Selig speaks to the media during a press conference prior to the game between the Seattle Mariners and the Houston Astros at Safeco Field on September 10, 2014, in Seattle, WA.*

RIGHT: *Pablo Sandoval #48 of the San Francisco Giants hits a single against the Kansas City Royals in the fourth inning during Game Five of the 2014 World Series at AT&T Park on October 26, 2014, in San Francisco, CA.*

WORLD SERIES
TOYOTA
YAHOO!
Adobe
PlayStation
GREATNESS AWAITS

B
Dodgers

BASEBALL GREATS

BASEBALL GREATS

HANK AARON

Hank Aaron is undoubtedly one of the most successful and most awarded outfielders in baseball history. Born on February 5, 1934, in Mobile, Alabama, Aaron was offered several football scholarships whilst at high school but turned them down to pursue a career in Major League Baseball.

On November 20, 1951, Aaron signed a contract with the Indianapolis Clowns, effectively starting his minor league career. Aaron helped the Clowns win the 1952 Negro League World Series and, as a result of his spectacular on-field performance during the series, he was offered two major league contracts: one from the New York Giants and one from the Boston Braves.

On June 14, 1952, Aaron signed with the Braves, who purchased him from the Clowns for US$10,000.

The Braves assigned Aaron to the Eau Claire Bears, their Northern League Class-C farm team. Playing in the infield, Aaron's skills developed substantially. He was elected to the Northern League's All-Star team for the first time and was unanimously voted the Rookie of the Year for the 1952 season.

Aaron was promoted to the Jacksonville Tars, the Braves' Class-A affiliate in the Salle League, in 1953. After leading the league in runs (115), hits (208), doubles (36), RBIs (125), total bases (338) and batting average (.352), Aaron debuted with the Braves' major league team on April 13, 1954. In 1956 he was voted *The Sporting News'* National League Player of the Year and in 1957 he was made National League MVP; he also helped the Braves win the 1957 World Series.

Over the next few years Aaron was in the prime of his career. On June 21, 1959, he hit three two-run home runs in a game against the San Francisco Giants, which was the first and only time that he hit three home runs in one game in his career. In 1963 he was the winner of the Double Crown after leading the National League with 44 home runs and 130 RBIs while finishing third in batting average. With 31 stolen bases and 44 home runs, Aaron became just the third player in history to steal 30 bases and hit 30 home runs in a single season. After the Braves moved from Milwaukee to Atlanta in 1965, Aaron continued to amass numerous home runs and successfully guarded the outfield.

Approaching the 1974 season Aaron's home run tally loomed on Babe Ruth's record of 714, causing widespread controversy.

Over the winter he received numerous death threats and hate mail from people who did not want to see a black man break Ruth's sacred home run tally. Despite the controversy, he tied Ruth's record in his very first at-bat in the 1974 season-opening series against the Cincinnati Reds and hit his 715th career home run against the LA Dodgers on April 8, 1974. The following year he also broke baseball's all-time RBI record. On July 20, 1976, he slugged his 755th and final home run, a major league record which was held for 33 years until Barry Bonds of the San Francisco Giants surpassed it on August 7, 2007.

Aaron played in his final major league game on October 3, 1976. At the conclusion of his 23-year career, he had hit 24 or more home runs every year from 1955 to 1973 and made the All-Star team every year from 1955 until 1975. He won three Rawlings Gold Glove Awards and holds the major league records for the most career RBIs (2,297), the most career extra base hits (1,477) and the most career total bases (6,856). He was also in the top five for career hits and runs.

Milwaukee Braves player Hank Aaron safe at home as Johnny Logan on one knee makes his own call of safe.

PLAYER STATISTICS:

Position:	Outfielder
Born:	February 5, 1934
Batted:	Right
Threw:	Right
HR:	755
AVG	.305
HR:	755
TBs:	6,856
RBI:	2,297
EBH:	1,477

TEAMS:

Milwaukee Braves (1954–1965)
Atlanta Braves (1966–1974)
Milwaukee Brewers (1975–1976)

HIGHLIGHTS/AWARDS:

- NL MVP (1957)
- 3x Gold Glove Award
- The Sporting News NL Player of the Year (1956, 1963)
- Lou Gehrig Memorial Award (1970)
- 25x All-Star
- World Series Winner (1957)

NOTEWORTHY:

- Holds second place on the career home run list, with 755 home runs
- Holds MLB record for most consecutive seasons with 150 or more hits (17)
- Member of the National Baseball Hall of Fame: Elected 1982, (Vote 97.83%, first ballot)

BASEBALL GREATS

JOHNNY BENCH

Catcher is arguably the most demanding position on the field. Normally, a catcher is either proficient offensively or they make things happen defensively; seldom is there a true complete package that spends his career behind the plate. As a top-flight catcher who did just that, Johnny Bench was one of the rarities.

Bench was drafted by the Cincinnati Reds in the second round of the 1965 MLB amateur draft as the 36th overall selection. He spent the 1966 and most of the 1967 seasons with the Buffalo Bisons in the minor leagues and made his major league debut on August 28, 1967, in a 3-2 Reds loss to the Philadelphia Phillies. He went 0-for-3 with two strikeouts in the game. Bench finished the 1967 season with a .163 batting average in 26 games spanning 86 at-bats, with one home run and six RBIs.

Bench came into camp in 1968 as the number one catcher on the roster, and he rewarded the Reds by playing in 154 games, hitting .275 with 40 doubles, 15 home runs and 82 RBIs. He was selected to the All-Star Game, won the Gold Glove for defensive excellence and was named the National League Rookie of the Year. This marked the first time the NL Rookie of the Year Award was given to a catcher, and also the first time a rookie won the Gold Glove.

Bench's numbers improved to a .293 average, 26 home runs and 90 RBIs during his second full season. Additionally, he won a second consecutive Gold Glove and was named to the All-Star Game. His greatest season was in 1970, in which he again hit .293 but also led the league, slamming 45 home runs and driving in 148 in the middle of Cincinnati's lineup. He claimed the NL MVP Award, at the time becoming the youngest player to do so at 22 years old, to go along with his third All-Star Game and Gold Glove selections. The Reds made the World Series but lost to the Baltimore Orioles.

Bench slumped to a .238 average in 1971 with 27 home runs and 61 RBIs, but returned with a vengeance in 1972. He bumped his average up to .270 while leading the league in home runs (40), RBIs (125), intentional walks (23) and sacrifice flies (12). He drew 100 walks on the season and scored 97 runs. Those numbers earned him his second NL MVP Award in three years, and he was selected as an All-Star and a Gold Glove recipient for the fifth consecutive season. The Reds fell short again in the World Series, losing to the Oakland Athletics.

Bench hit 25 home runs and drove in 104 during the 1973 season but the Reds fell apart in the playoffs. In 1974 he became the fourth catcher in history to score 100 runs and drive in 100 in the same season, as he batted .280 with 33 home runs, a league-leading 129 RBIs and 108 runs scored, which was a career high. He also led the NL in total bases with 315.

The Reds, known as the Big Red Machine, were rolling in the mid-1970s. Bench was a major cog in that engine, smacking 28 home runs and driving in 110 during the 1975 season. The Reds claimed the World Series in 1975, defeating the Red Sox in a thrilling series well remembered for Game Six, with Boston getting timely home runs from Bernie Carbo and then Carlton Fisk to force a Game Seven.

Cincinnati repeated as World Series Champions in 1976 and is the most recent team to win back-to-back NL championships. Bench hit just .234 with 16 home runs and 74 RBIs during the regular season but rebounded to hit .533 (8 of 15) with two home runs in the World Series, and he was awarded the World Series MVP. He hit .275 with 31 home runs and 109 RBIs during the 1977 season, which was his last season with 100 or more RBIs.

Bench finished his career with a .267 batting average, 389 home runs and 1376 RBIs over 2158 games. He was a two-time NL MVP, a World Series MVP, was selected to the All-Star Game 14 times, won 10 Gold Glove Awards, and led the league in home runs twice and RBIs on three occasions. The Reds retired his number five in 1984, and he was inducted into the Baseball Hall of Fame in his first year of eligibility in 1989.

Catcher Johnny Bench of the Cincinnati Reds.

PLAYER STATISTICS:
Position: Catcher
Born: December 7, 1947
Batted: Right
Threw: Right
Hits: 2048
AVG: 267
HR: 389
RBI: 1,376
EBH: 794
TEAMS:
Cincinnati Reds (1967-1983)
HIGHLIGHTS/AWARDS:
• National League Rookie of the Year (1968)
• 10x Gold Glove Award (1968-1977)
• 2x NL MVP (1970, 1972)
• 14x All-Star (1968-1980, 1983)
• Lou Gehrig Award (1975)
• World Series MVP (1976)
• Babe Ruth Award (1976)
• Hutch Award (1981)
NOTEWORTHY:
• Led NL in Total Bases (315) in 1974
• Twice led NL in Home Runs (1970, 972)
• Led NL in RBI 3 times (1970, 1972, 1974)
• Twice led NL in Extra-Base Hits (1970, 1974)
• Led NL in Sacrifice Flies 3 times (1970, 1972-73)
• Led NL in Intentional Walks (23) in 1972
• Member of the National Baseball Hall of Fame: Elected 1989 (Vote 96.42%)

BASEBALL GREATS
YOGI BERRA

Like Bench, Lawrence Peter "Yogi" Berra is widely regarded as one of the greatest catchers in baseball history. Following service in the US Army during the Second World War, Berra began playing with the Newark Bears in the minor leagues before being called up by the New York Yankees, making his major league debut on September 22, 1946. He played just seven games for the Yankees in 1946, but by the following year he became a permanent player in the Yankees lineup and an integral part of the Yankees domination throughout his 19-year career.

Berra's great speed, athleticism and quick reflexes made him an outstanding fielder and catcher. He led the American League for catchers eight times in games caught and in chances accepted. He also topped the league six times in double plays (a major league record), eight times in putouts, three times in assists and once in fielding percentage. Upon his retirement, he took the American League records for the most catcher putouts (8,738) and chances accepted (9,520). He was also one of only one of four catchers to go an entire season without making an error, which he achieved in 1958. In the middle of the 1962 season, Berra, who was then 37 years of age, demonstrated his tremendous physical endurance by catching an entire 22-inning, seven-hour match against the Detroit Tigers.

As well as being a superb catcher, Berra was also an accomplished batter and feared clutch hitter. He had the special skill of being able to adapt instantaneously to hit bad pitches from all areas of the strike zone and beyond. Whether it was swinging at low pitches to produce deep home runs or chopping at high pitches for line dives, Berra's versatility at bat made him a threatening all-rounder. Berra also had great control and extension. In five seasons he hit more home runs than strikeouts, notably in 1950 when he struck out only 12 times in 597 at-bats.

During his career with the Yankees, Berra appeared in a record 14 World Series championships, 10 of which the Yankees won, and a total of 75 World Series games, a major league record. He also established World Series records for the most at-bats (259), hits (71), doubles (10), singles (49), games caught (63) and catcher putouts (457). Additionally, Berra hit the first pinch-hit home run in World Series history during Game Three of the 1947 World Series against the Brooklyn Dodgers.

On top of his World Series achievements, Berra appeared in 15 All-Star games and received MVP votes in every year of his career, winning the award three times, in 1951, 1954 and 1955. For seven consecutive years, from 1949 to 1955, Berra led the Yankees in RBIs.

After the 1963 World Series, Berra ceased his playing career with the New York Yankees but was hired as the team manager for the 1964 season. He briefly returned as a player-coach for the New York Mets in 1965 but played in only four games, with his last official major league game coming on May 9, 1965. He went on to coach the Mets for the next eight years and in 1972 was admitted to the Baseball Hall of Fame. *The Sporting News* ranked Berra No. 40 on the list of 100 Greatest Baseball Players of all time in 1999 and soon after he was named as second catcher in the Major League Baseball All-Century Team, receiving 704,208 ballots.

Yogi Berra, catcher for for the New York Yankees, swinging the bat during a game, 1950s.

PLAYER STATISTICS:

Position: Catcher/Manager
Born: May 12, 1925
Batted: Left
Threw: Right
HR: 358
AVG: .285
RBI: 1430

TEAMS:

New York Yankees (1946-1963)
New York Mets (1965)

HIGHLIGHTS/AWARDS:

- 3x AL MVP (1951, 1954, 1955)
- 18x AL All-star (1948-1962)

NOTEWORTHY:

- Member of the National Baseball Hall of Fame: Elected 1972 (Vote 85.61%, second ballot)

BASEBALL GREATS
ROGER CLEMENS

The starting pitcher for the New York Yankees, William Roger Clemens, nicknamed "Rocket," is one of the finest and most accomplished major league pitchers in history. A right-handed pitcher and batter, Clemens launched his career with the Boston Red Sox after being drafted as the 19th overall pick in 1983. He quickly escalated through the minor league system and was unveiled in the major leagues the following year. His 24 wins during the 1986 season helped take the Red Sox to the 1986 World Series, and he was named the 1986 American League MVP and also won his first Cy Young Award. During that season, he also became the first pitcher to strike out 20 batters in a nine-inning major league game. Ten years later on September 18, 1996, against the Detroit Tigers, Clemens accomplished the 20-strikeout feat for the second time, to date the only player ever to do so. The 1996 season was his last season with the Red Sox, and he finished his time in Boston with 192 wins, tied with Cy Young for the club record.

Prior to the 1997 season Clemens signed with the Toronto Blue Jays. He won the Cy Young Award again in 1997 and 1998 as well as the Triple Crown in both years. Despite what many believe were Clemens's best individual seasons of his career, he was traded to the Yankees before the start of the 1999 season and helped them win the World Series that year. He was also ranked number 53 on *The Sporting News*' list of Baseball's 100 Greatest Players and was elected to the All-Century Team. The Yankees won the 2000 World Series title and the following year Clemens became the first pitcher in history to start off a season with a 20-1 win-loss record. He finished 2001 at 20-3 and won his sixth Cy Young Award.

In 2003 Clemens announced his retirement from professional baseball, effective at the end of that season. He recorded his 300th career win and 4,000th career strikeout on June 13, 2003, against the Cardinals; he is the only player in history to record both milestones in the same game. By the end of the 2003 season Clemens was met with a series of public farewells, and in the World Series against the Florida Marlins, Clemens left his final game trailing 3-1 after seven innings. Prior to the start of the 2004 season, however, Clemens decided to play on and signed a one-year deal with the Houston Astros. He finished the 2004 season with 4,317 career strikeouts, the second-highest of all time behind Nolan Ryan, and his 18-4 record gave him a career record of 328-164. At the age of 42, he received his seventh Cy Young Award, the oldest player to ever win the award.

Clemens signed a lucrative $18 million one-year contract with the Astros for 2005, which was the highest annual salary ever earned by a major league pitcher at the time. It proved to be an excellent season for Clemens, who won 13 games while leading the National League with a 1.87 ERA and finished in third place in Cy Young Award voting. He participated in the 2006 World Baseball Classic and continued playing with the Astros for the remainder of the 2006 season, when he was named in *Sports Illustrated*'s "all-time" team.

He returned to the Yankees for the 2007 season and on June 21, 2007, at the age of 44, he became the oldest Yankee to record a hit. On July 2, 2007, he received his 350th win in a 5-1 victory against the Minnesota Twins. On August 18, 2007, Clemens recorded his 1,000th strikeout with the Yankees, the ninth player in major league history to get 1,000 or more strikeouts with two different teams. He will be remembered as one of the greatest pitchers of all time with the second-most career wins for a right-handed pitcher during the live-ball era.

Because he successfully pitched just as good in his 40s as he did in his 20s, Clemens finished his career under suspicion of using performance-enhancing drugs.

New York Yankees starting pitcher Roger Clemens looks towards home plate after giving up a 2-run home run. Clemens pitched 7 1/3 innings before leaving the game. He picked up his fifth loss as the A's went on to win 6-1.

PLAYER STATISTICS:

Position: Pitcher
Born: August 4, 1962
Bats: Right
Throws: Right
Win-Loss: 354-184
ERA: 3.12
SO: 4,672

TEAMS:

Boston Red Sox (1984-1996)
Toronto Blue Jays (1997-1998)
New York Yankees (1999-2003)
Houston Astros (2004-2006)
New York Yankees (2007)

BASEBALL GREATS

TY COBB

Known as the Georgia Peach, Ty Cobb was one of baseball's greatest hitters. He was also one of the sport's most controversial players due to his cantankerous attitude, penchant for lashing out, and blatant racist mentality. To say he was a polarizing figure would be a gross understatement. Despite his personal shortcomings, Cobb is widely accepted as one of the greatest players in major league history.

Cobb made his major league debut for the Detroit Tigers on August 30, 1905, just three weeks after he suffered the tragedy of his mother fatally shooting his father. He hit just .240 in 41 games that season, but it was enough to earn a fairly lucrative $1,500 contract for the next season. Cobb would hit .316 in his first season as a regular in 1906, stealing 23 bases in 98 games. He would never hit for an average that low again in the rest of his career.

The Tigers won three straight AL pennants in 1907, 1908 and 1909, but they failed to translate that success into a World Series victory. Cobb led the league in hitting all three seasons, as well as in hits and RBIs all three years. He claimed the Triple Crown in 1909, hitting a robust .337 with 9 home runs, 107 RBIs and 76 stolen bases. He became the only player in major league history to lead the league in home runs without hitting a ball over the fence; all of them were inside the park.

Cobb won the AL MVP Award in 1911 after leading the league in almost every offensive category: he scored 147 runs, had 248 hits, 47 doubles, 24 triples, drove in 127 runs, stole 83 bases, hit .420, had a slugging percentage of .621, an OPS of 1.088 and had 367 total bases. He only finished second to Frank "Home Run" Baker in home runs. That was the first of five straight batting titles for Cobb through 1915. He would eventually win 11, all of them coming in a 13-year span from 1907 through 1919.

Cobb is the only major league player to have two 35-game hitting streaks in his career, posting a 40-game streak in 1911 and following it up with a 35-game run in 1915. He had six hitting streaks in at least 20 games in his career, second all-time to Pete Rose's seven. Cobb spent 67 days in the United States Army Chemical Corps and was honorably discharged in 1918. He became the youngest player in history to reach 3,000 hits on August 19, 1921, with a hit off Elmer Meyers of the Red Sox. Cobb accomplished this in the fewest at-bats, having needed just 8,093.

Cobb took over as manager of the Tigers in 1921 and would be a player-manager for the team for the next six seasons. The Tigers never seriously threatened for a pennant, and a third-place finish in 1924 was their best showing under his guidance. Cobb finished with a record of 479-444 as manager and blamed his difficulties on the lack of spending by ownership. He finished his career with the Tigers in 1926 and signed with the Philadelphia Athletics in 1927.

He doubled in his first at-bat back in Detroit as a member of the A's, and would record his 4,000th career hit on July 19, 1927. Cobb played less frequently in 1928 due to his advancing age, and his final hit came against the Washington Senators on September 3, 1928, when he doubled off Bump Hadley. Cobb retired at the end of the season, finishing with 23 consecutive seasons where he hit at least .300, a mark that is unlikely to ever be matched.

Cobb finished his career with 4,191 hits, a career batting average of .366 (which is the best in the history of the game), 724 doubles, 295 triples, 117 home runs, 1938 RBIs, 897 stolen bases, 1249 walks and just 680 strikeouts in 13,077 at-bats. He won 11 batting titles, led the league in runs-scored five times, in triples four times, in RBIs four times and in steals in five separate seasons. Seven times he drove in at least 100 runs, and 11 times he scored at least 100 times. Cobb was inducted into the Baseball Hall of Fame in 1936 after being named on 98.2 percent of the ballots. He died on July 17, 1961, at the age of 74.

Full-length image of Detroit outfielder Ty Cobb (1886 - 1961) touching third base while running during a baseball game.

PLAYER STATISTICS:

Position: Outfielder
Born: December 18, 1886
Died: July 17, 1961 (aged 74)
Batted: Left
Threw: Right
Hits: 4191
AVG: .367
RBI: 1938

TEAMS:

Detroit Tigers (Player 1905–1926)
Philadelphia Athletics (Player 1927–1928)
Detroit Tigers (Manager 1921–1926)

HIGHLIGHTS/AWARDS:

Career batting average (.366) [1]
Career steals of home (54)
Career batting titles (11 or 12) [1]

NOTEWORTHY:

- Batted over .320 for 22 straight seasons
- Batted over .400 three times (1911, 1912 & 1922)
- Won the Triple Crown in 1909
- One of the inaugural members of the Hall of Fame
- Member of the National Baseball Hall of Fame: Elected 1936 (Vote 98.2%)

BASEBALL GREATS

JOE DIMAGGIO

There may not be a more iconic player in the storied history of the New York Yankees than the Yankee Clipper himself, Joe DiMaggio. He led the Yankees to nine World Series championships in his 13 seasons in the majors, and his numbers would have been even more impressive had he not missed three seasons during World War II. DiMaggio came from a family well-versed in Major League Baseball, as his brothers Vince and Dom both were All-Stars during their careers.

DiMaggio was playing for the San Francisco Seals in the Pacific Coast League when the Yankees acquired him on December 19, 1934. They sent Doc Farrell, Floyd Newkirk, Jim Densmore, Ted Norbert and $5,000 to the Seals for DiMaggio. The Seals kept DiMaggio for the 1935 season and he led the club to the PCL title, winning the PCL MVP Award for his efforts.

DiMaggio made his debut for the Yankees on May 3, 1936, and finished 3-for-6 with a triple, two singles, three runs scored and a run batted in as the Yankees defeated the St. Louis Browns 14-5. In his first season, he would finish with a .323 batting average, 132 runs scored, 206 hits, and a league-leading 15 triples, 29 home runs and 125 RBIs. He was named to the All-Star Team, and the Yankees claimed their first championship since 1932 in six games over the New York Giants.

In 1937 DiMaggio put together a tremendous season, leading the league in runs scored (151), total bases (418), slugging percentage (.673) and home runs (46), while driving in 167 runs, collecting 215 hits and posting a .346 batting average. All of that was only good for second place in the MVP race, and the award went to Detroit's Charlie Gehringer instead. DiMaggio did not claim his first MVP Award until 1939, when he won his first of two batting titles with a .381 average to go along with 30 home runs and 126 RBIs.

With a .352 average, DiMaggio won his second batting title in 1940, but the season that everyone talks about is 1941. Much like the summer of 1998 was all about Mark McGwire and Sammy Sosa, 1941 featured Joe DiMaggio and Ted Williams. Williams hit .406 and is the last man in baseball history to reach the hallowed ground of .400 in one season. Meanwhile, DiMaggio broke Wee Willie Keeler's mark of 44 consecutive games with a base hit with his own 56-game streak. The streak began on May 15, 1941, and ended on July 17 when the Cleveland Indians held DiMaggio without a hit, helped by two defensive plays by third baseman Ken Keltner.

After the streak ended, DiMaggio hit in 17 consecutive games, giving him hits in 73 of 74 games. He finished the year with a .357 average, 30 home runs and a league-best 125 RBIs. He also had 193 hits, 43 doubles, 11 triples and 122 runs scored. When the MVP votes were tallied, DiMaggio had edged Williams by 37 points to claim his second award. Both players achieved feats that have not been challenged or broken since.

DiMaggio missed the 1943, 1944 and 1945 seasons during World War II after he enlisted in the Army Air Forces. He attained the rank of sergeant and received a medical discharge in September 1945 due to chronic stomach ulcers. He returned to baseball in 1946 but the rust of not playing showed. After driving in at least 114 runs in each of his first seven seasons, DiMaggio drove in more than 100 runs just twice in his final six years. He claimed his third MVP Award in 1947, edging Williams by one point.

In 1951 DiMaggio had his worst season statistically, hitting just .263 with 12 home runs and 71 RBIs, and he announced his retirement on December 11, 1951. He was named to the All-Star Game in each of his 13 seasons. He won two batting titles and three MVP Awards, leading the league in home runs twice, total bases three times, RBIs twice, slugging percentage twice, runs scored once and triples once. The Yankees retired his number five in 1952, and he was inducted into the Baseball Hall of Fame in 1955. He died on March 8, 1999, at the age of 84 due to lung cancer.

New York Yankees outfielder Joe DiMaggio (1914 - 1999) poses in uniform while holding several bats.

PLAYER STATISTICS:

Position: Center Fielder
Born: November 25, 1914
Died: March 8, 1999 (aged 84)
Batted: Right
Threw: Right
Hits: 2214
AVG: .325
HR: 361

TEAMS:
New York Yankees (1936-1942, 1946-1951)

HIGHLIGHTS/AWARDS:
- 3x AL MVP (1939, 1941, 1947)

NOTEWORTHY:
- Member of the National Baseball Hall of Fame: Elected 1955, (Vote 88.84% third ballot: first eligible in 1953)
- Led league in batting average 1939 (.381) & 1940 (.352)
- Led league in slugging percentage 1937 (.673) & 1950 (.585)
- Led league in runs 1937 (151)
- Led league in total bases 1937 (418), 1941 (348) & 1948 (355)
- Led league in triples 1936 (15)
- Led league in home runs 1937 (46) & 1948 (39)
- Led league in RBIs 1941 (125) & 1948 (155)
- Led league in extra-base hits 1941 (84) & 1950 (75)
- Led league in At Bats per Home Run 1948 (15.2)
- Had at least one hit in 56 consecutive games.

BASEBALL GREATS

LOU GEHRIG

The nickname "The Iron Horse" was a prophetic one for Lou Gehrig. From 1925 through 1939 Gehrig was in the lineup for every Yankees game, playing in a then-record 2,130 consecutive games. That record would last 56 years until Cal Ripken Jr. broke it in 1995. Gehrig was part of a tremendous era in Yankees baseball, and one has to wonder what more he could have done had he not been pushed out of the sport by the disease that would eventually kill him at the age of 37.

Gehrig was signed as an amateur free agent by the Yankees in 1923. He initially played in the minor leagues at Hartford and tore up opposing pitching, hitting .344 with 61 home runs in 193 contests. He made his major league debut as a pinch-hitter in a Yankees 10-0 win over the St. Louis Browns on June 15, 1923, but he didn't fully break into the lineup until 1925.

Gehrig's ironman streak began on June 1, 1925, when he entered the game as a pinch-hitter for Paul Wanninger. The next day, he was in the lineup at first base to replace Wally Pipp, who was in a miserable slump. This swap was one of several moves by Miller Huggins to shake the ball club up. Gehrig finished the year playing in 126 games, hitting .295 with 20 home runs and 68 RBIs. This was a precursor of what was to come from the Yankees first baseman.

The 1926 season served as Gehrig's breakout year and notice to the rest of the league that he had arrived. He finished the year hitting .313 with 47 doubles, a league-best 20 triples, 16 home runs and 112 RBIs. In 1927, as part of the Murderers' Row lineup that saw Babe Ruth slam 60 home runs and four players drive in more than 100 runs, Gehrig stood out among the other titans that wore pinstripes. He would score 149 runs, collect 218 hits, a league-leading 52 doubles, 18 triples, 47 home runs and a league-best 175 RBIs. The Yankees swept the Pittsburgh Pirates to claim the World Series, and Gehrig earned his first MVP Award.

Gehrig would continue his torrid offensive numbers, leading the league in RBIs four times in five years from 1927 through 1931. He had six seasons where he batted .350 or better (with a high of .379 in 1930), plus a seventh season at .349. He had seven seasons with 150 or more RBIs, 11 seasons with over 100 walks, eight seasons with 200 or more hits, and five seasons with more than 40 home runs. Gehrig led the AL in runs scored four times, home runs three times, and RBIs five times. His 184 RBIs in 1931 remain the AL record as of 2014 and rank second all-time to Hack Wilson's 191 RBIs in 1930.

Despite Gehrig leading the league in most offensive categories in 1931, including runs scored (163), hits (211), home runs (46), RBIs (184), total bases (410) and plate appearances (738), he only finished second in the MVP voting. Philadelphia pitcher Lefty Grove claimed the award with a 31-4 record and a 2.04 ERA. A similar situation unfolded in 1934, when Gehrig led the league in home runs (49), RBIs (165), batting average (.363), on-base percentage (.465), slugging percentage (.706), OPS (1.172) and total bases (409), yet finished fifth.

Gehrig's ironman streak came to an end in 1939. His prodigious power was gone, and his coordination and speed were dissipating as well. On May 2, 1939, he told manager Joe McCarthy that he was taking himself out of the lineup for the good of the team. McCarthy told Gehrig that his position was his whenever he chose to return, but Gehrig never played again.

After a series of tests at the Mayo Clinic in Minnesota, Gehrig was diagnosed with amyotrophic lateral sclerosis on June 19, 1939, his 36th birthday. The Yankees announced Gehrig's retirement two days later and in a major league first, retired his number four. Gehrig was inducted into the Baseball Hall of Fame in 1939 by special election, and finished his career with a .340 batting average, 1888 runs scored, 2721 hits, 493 home runs, and 1995 RBIs. Sixteen years to the day of replacing Wally Pipp, Gehrig died at the age of 37 on June 2, 1941.

First baseman Lou Gehrig #4 of the New York Yankees takes batting practice at the Polo Grounds before the beginning of the 1937 World Series with the New York Giants.

PLAYER STATISTICS:

Position:	First Baseman
Born:	June 19, 1903
Died:	June 2, 1941 (aged 37)
Batted:	Left
Threw:	Left
AVG:	.340 (2,721-for-8,001)
HR:	493
RBI:	1,995
GSH:	23

TEAMS:
New York Yankees (1923-1939)

HIGHLIGHTS/AWARDS:
- 2x AL MVP (1927, 1936)
- Triple Crown (1934) Led the league in batting average (.363), home runs (49), and RBIs (165)

NOTEWORTHY:
- Member of the National Baseball Hall of Fame Elected 1939 (Vote Unanimous)
- Played in 2,130 consecutive games: June 1, 1925 to April 30, 1939
- Highest Career Slugging Percentage by a First Baseman: .632
- 7x All-Star: 1933-1939 (DNP 1939)
- Led the league in home runs: 1931 (46), 1934 (49) & 1936 (49)
- Led the league in RBIs: 1927 (175), 1928 (142), 1930 (174), 1931 (184) & 1934 (165)
- Led the league in times on base: 1927 (330), 1930 (324), 1931 (328), 1934 (321), 1936 (342) & 1937 (331)

BASEBALL GREATS

BOB GIBSON

A classic power pitcher, Bob Gibson spent 17 years in the major leagues making the lives of hitters extremely difficult. He could pitch, field his position, and even swing the bat with some authority, a rarity for most pitchers. He delayed his baseball career by a season so he could play basketball with the Harlem Globetrotters, but when he focused on baseball, he was the ace the Cardinals' rotation needed.

The Cardinals signed Gibson as an amateur free agent before the 1957 season and gave him a $3,000 bonus. He began his career in 1958 in the minors and made his major league debut on April 15, 1959, in relief of starter Larry Jackson. Gibson allowed two runs on two hits in two innings of work as the Cardinals lost 5-0 to the Los Angeles Dodgers.

Gibson briefly pitched for Omaha in the minors and was recalled as a starting pitcher on July 30. He went the distance in his first start, scattering eight hits in a 1-0 victory over the Cincinnati Reds. He finished the 1959 season with a 3-5 record along with a 3.33 ERA in 13 games, nine of which were starts. Over the course of 75.2 innings, he allowed 77 hits, walked 39 and struck out 48 hitters. The 1960 season similarly saw Gibson shuffling between the bullpen and the rotation. He was 3-6 with a 5.61 ERA in 27 games, 12 of which were starts. This continued into the first half of 1961 under manager Solly Hemus, who was not a fan of Gibson. In July 1961 Hemus was replaced with Johnny Keane, who had been the manager in Omaha. He quickly installed Gibson in the starting rotation and was rewarded: Gibson went 13-12 with a 3.24 ERA in 35 games, 27 starts and threw a total of 211.1 innings. Gibson had control issues, but better days were ahead. He would make his first All-Star team in 1962, going 15-13 with a 2.85 ERA over 233.2 innings and posted a league-leading five shutouts.

The 1963 season was Gibson's breakout year. He went 18-9 with a 3.39 ERA with 14 complete games and a pair of shutouts. This was the first year that the strike zone was expanded to above the belt of hitters, benefitting pitchers across the league. In 1964 Gibson went 19-12 with a 3.01 ERA, as the Cardinals roared back from an 11-game deficit on August 23, and a six-and-a-half game hole on September 20. Gibson and the Cardinals went 10-3 down the stretch to claim the pennant, and then they outlasted the Yankees in the World Series with Gibson setting a record with 31 strikeouts.

Gibson posted the first of five 20-win seasons in 1965, going 20-12 with a 3.07 ERA. He also made the All-Star Game and won the first of nine consecutive Gold Glove Awards. He won his 20th game on the final day of the season with most of the regulars out of the lineup, defeating the Houston Astros 5-2. That was followed by a 21-win season in 1966, but an injury marred 1967 and he won just 13 games in the regular season. Gibson missed nearly two months with a broken leg after he was hit with a line drive off the bat of Roberto Clemente on July 15. He would not return until September 7, but the Cardinals claimed the pennant. In the World Series, he threw three complete game victories as the Cardinals defeated the Red Sox for their second title in four years. Gibson's best year was yet to come, however.

The 1968 season was known as the "Year of the Pitcher." Denny McLain of the Detroit Tigers won 31 games, and to date is the last pitcher to reach the hallowed ground of 30 victories in a season. In the National League, Gibson went 22-9 with a live-ball era record low ERA of 1.12 over 308.2 innings of work. Gibson was the winner in Games One and Four of the World Series against the Tigers, but lost Game Seven 4-1, giving the Series to the Tigers.

Gibson would win 20 games in 1969 and a league-leading and career-best 23 games in 1970. He finished his career with a record of 251-174 with a 2.91 ERA in 528 games, 482 of which were starts. He logged 255 complete games, 56 shutouts, and 3,117 strikeouts in his career.

St Louis Cardinals player Bob Gibson in a photo signing autographs.

PLAYER STATISTICS:

Position: Pitcher
Born: November 9, 1935
Batted: Right
Threw: Right
Win-Loss 251-174
ERA: 2.91
Strikeouts 3,117

TEAMS:

St. Louis Cardinals (1959-1975)

HIGHLIGHTS/AWARDS:

- National League MVP (1968)
- 2x World Series MVP (1964, 1967)
- 9x All-Star (1962, 1965-70, 1972)
- 9x Gold Glove Award (1965-1973)
- 2x Cy Young Award (1968, 1970)

NOTEWORTHY:

- Member of the National Baseball Hall of Fame: Elected 1981 (Vote 84.0%, first ballot)
- ERA of 1.12 in 1968 is major league best in the Live Ball Era, 2nd best all-time ERA.
- Seven World Series Wins
- Record for most strikeouts during a World Series (35 Ks in 1968)
- Record for most strikeouts in a World Series game (17 Ks in Game One, 1968)

BASEBALL GREATS

KEN GRIFFEY JR.

The American League's Seattle Mariners selected Ken Griffey Jr. as the first overall pick of the 1987 Major League Baseball draft. He made his major league debut on April 3, 1989, and was on his way to securing the Rookie of the Year Award when he slipped and broke his right hand. Once his hand mended, Griffey became a regular fixture with the Mariners and in 1990 and 1991 became one of a handful of players to play on the same team as his father, Ken Griffey Sr.

Griffey went on to establish himself as one of baseball's leading players during the 1990s. He was one of the leading runs scorers of the decade and slugged 422 home runs in the 1990s. Griffey also became known as one of the greatest defensive players in the league. In center field he frequently made spectacular diving plays and entertained fans with over-the-shoulder basket catches or by saving potential home runs at the wall, leaping up and pulling big hits back into the field of play. With the Mariners, Griffey led the league numerous times in hitting categories and was awarded the Gold Glove for his defensive brilliance from 1990 to 1999. He was the 1992 All-Star Game MVP and in 1997 he was awarded the American League MVP. In 1999 he was ranked 93rd on *The Sporting News'* list of the 100 Greatest Baseball Players of all time and was also elected to the Major League Baseball All-Century Team.

At the end of the 1999 season, Griffey was traded to the Cincinnati Reds. The 2000 season was the start of a decline in his superstar status that he had created during the previous decade, however. He hit .271 with 40 home runs, but his on-base/slugging percentage of .942 was the lowest in five years. From 2001 to 2004 Griffey was plagued by a series of injuries, cutting his seasons short in 2002, 2003 and 2004. Just prior to rupturing his right hamstring on August 4, 2004, Griffey recorded his 500th career home run on June 20, becoming the 20th player to do so in the history of Major League Baseball.

By the start of the 2005 season, Griffey returned to the Cincinnati lineup fitter, and he seemingly had left his injuries behind him. In early September, however, he strained a tendon in his left foot and the Reds decided to rest him for the remainder of the season so he could have surgery. Despite this, he was named the National League Comeback Player of the Year. The 2006 season proved to be better for Griffey, and on September 25, 2006, he hit his 27th home run of the season to tie Reggie Jackson for 10th on the all-time home run list with a total of 563 career home runs.

Before the start of the 2007 season Griffey's unfortunate injury streak returned when he broke his wrist whilst playing with his children, but he recovered in time for the start of the season. He would reach the 600 home run club on June 9, 2008, against the Florida Marlins. A few weeks later he was traded to the Chicago White Sox with hopes of finally winning a World Series title. For the 2009 season Griffey returned to Seattle, where he slugged 18 home runs for 629 for his career—just 31 behind Willie Mays for fifth place all time.

Griffey returned to the Mariners for the 2010 campaign with a similar contract to that of 2009. On June 2, 2010, weeks after being taken out of the lineup due to a lack of productivity, Ken Griffey released a statement through the Seattle Mariners organization announcing his retirement from Major League Baseball effective immediately. Griffey retired fifth on the all-time home run list.

Ken Griffey Jr #24 of the Seattle Mariners swings at the pitch during the game against the San Francisco Giants on May 24, 2009, at Safeco Field in Seattle, WA.

PLAYER STATISTICS:

Position: Center fielder
Born: November 21, 1969
Bats: Left
Throws: Left
Avg: .284
HR: 630
RBI: 1,836

TEAMS:

Seattle Mariners (1989-1999)
Cincinnati Reds (2000-2007)
Chicago White Sox (2007-2008)
Seattle Mariners (2009-2010)
Major League Baseball All-Century Team

BASEBALL GREATS

ROGERS HORNSBY

Rogers Hornsby was a solid second baseman, shortstop, third baseman and manager in the major leagues for 38 years. Starting his baseball career at the age of 18 as a shortstop in the Texas-Oklahoma League in 1914, Hornsby was soon offered a $500 contract by the St Louis Cardinals. He debuted in the major league on September 10, 1915, and went on to hit .246 in his rookie year. By 1917 he was topping the National League in slugging, total bases and double plays, and was second overall in batting. Two years later he was moved to third base position and again finished second in the National League batting ranks. The 1920 season was Hornsby's first full season as a second baseman. He topped the league in putouts, assists and double plays whilst leading the league in batting and RBIs. He capped off his impressive season by hitting a .370 batting average, the highest in the twentieth century by a National League second baseman.

Over the next five years while playing with the Cardinals, Hornsby not only matched his solid batting average but he improved it, continuing to lead the league for all five seasons in batting average, on-base percentage and slugging percentage. He hit .397, .401, .384, .424 and .403 consecutively, making him the only player in history to average over .400 for a five-year span. In 1922 he became the first National League player to hit 40 home runs in a single season. In 1927 Hornsby moved over to the New York Giants before signing as a player-manager for the Boston Braves in 1928 and the Chicago Cubs from 1929 to 1932. In 1933 he moved back to St. Louis and was player-manager for the Cardinals and the St. Louis Browns before playing out his last three seasons solely for the Browns. He played in his last major league game on July 20, 1937.

During his 15 seasons as a full-time player, Hornsby finished in the top four in batting average 12 times. He currently holds the second-highest career batting average of .358, the highest for any right-handed hitter or National League player. He also holds the modern record for the highest batting average in a single season, which he achieved in 1924 with .424. In total, Hornsby won seven batting crowns while finishing as runner-up three times, two home run crowns, and four RBI titles. He also led the league in slugging average nine times and was runner-up on two other occasions. Hornsby holds a major league record of 13 consecutive games with two or more base hits, achieved from July 5 through to July 18, 1923.

Hornsby hit an impressive 301 career home runs and is among the top four in home runs by a second baseman. He finished with a career average of 3.31 assists per game and is the seventh highest of any second baseman in baseball history. He won the Triple Crown twice, in 1922 and 1925, and also won the National League MVP Award twice, in 1925 and 1929; in 1942 he was inducted to the Baseball Hall of Fame. After his playing career, Hornsby was made full-time manager of the St. Louis Browns in 1952 before taking on the role with the Cincinnati Reds for the end of the 1952 and 1953 season. In 1963 Rogers Hornsby passed away from a heart attack after cataract surgery.

In 1999 *The Sporting News'* list of the 100 Greatest Baseball Players of all time ranked him as number 9, the highest-ranked second baseman. Later that year he was elected to the Major League Baseball All-Century Team with 630,767 votes.

Hall of Fame infielder and manager Rogers Hornsby of the Chicago Cubs pauses for a photo in the dugout at Wrigley Field in Chicago, IL.

PLAYER STATISTICS:

Position:	Second Baseman
Born:	April 27, 1896
Died:	January 5, 1963 (aged 66)
Batted:	Right
Threw:	Right
AVG:	.358
Hits:	2930
HR:	301

TEAMS:

St. Louis Cardinals	Player (1915-1926, 1933)
	Manager (1925-1926)
New York Giants	Player (1927)
	Manager (1927)
Boston Braves	Player (1928)
	Manager (1928)
Chicago Cubs	Player (1929-1932)
	Manager (1930-1932)
St. Louis Browns	Player (1933-1937)
	Manager (1933-1937, 1952)
Cincinnati Reds	Manager (1952-1953)

HIGHLIGHTS/AWARDS:

- Won seven batting titles, two HR titles and four RBI crowns.
- Won triple crowns in 1922 and 1925.
- Holds the NL record for career batting average at .358.

NOTEWORTHY:

- Member of the National Baseball Hall of Fame: Elected 1942 (Vote 78.1%, first ballot)
- Hornsby is the only player in history to average a .400 batting average over a 5 year span (1921-25).
- Rogers' .424 batting average in 1924 is the highest mark in the NL in the 20th century.

BASEBALL GREATS

DEREK JETER

For nearly two decades, Derek Jeter was a cornerstone of the New York Yankees lineup. Jeter was drafted with the sixth overall pick in the 1992 MLB Draft by the Yankees. He was heavily sought after by the Astros but the management of the franchise worried that Jeter would demand a seven-figure signing bonus in order to give up going to college and instead chose Phil Nevin. Jeter took an $800,000 bonus to sign with the Yankees.

Jeter went 0-for-7 with five strikeouts in his professional debut and ended up hitting just .202 in 47 games on the season. He was called up to Single-A Greensboro in the South Atlantic League where he played in 11 games.

In 1993, Jeter's first full season in professional baseball, he improved his offensive numbers as he hit .295 with 14 doubles, 11 triples, five home runs, 71 RBIs and 18 steals. In 1994 Jeter advanced from Tampa in the Florida State League to Columbus in Triple A. He was named the Minor League Player of the Year by *Baseball America*, *The Sporting News* and *USA Today*.

Jeter spent the majority of the 1995 season at Triple-A Columbus. He played 123 games for the Clippers, hitting .317 with 27 doubles, 9 triples, 2 home runs, 45 RBIs and 20 steals. He made his major league debut for the Yankees on May 29, 1995; he went 0-for-5 with a strikeout against the Mariners in an 8-7, 12-inning defeat. He would get his first career hit a day later with a single in a 7-3 loss.

Jeter won the AL Rookie of the Year Award in 1996 as he played in 157 games on the season. He hit .314 with 183 hits, 25 doubles, 6 triples, 10 homers, 78 RBIs and 14 stolen bases while scoring 104 runs. Jeter hit .324 with 203 hits, a league-leading 127 runs, 25 doubles, 8 triples, 19 home runs, 84 RBIs and 30 steals in 1998.

In 2000 Jeter hit a solid .339 with 201 hits, 31 doubles, four triples, 15 homers, 73 RBIs and 22 steals. He was again named to the All-Star Game. He hit .317 in 16 postseason games, slamming four home runs and driving in nine runs as the Yankees won their third straight World Series championship. That was followed up by a .311 mark in 2001 as he scored 110 runs, banged out 191 hits, 35 doubles, 3 triples, 21 home runs, 74 RBIs and 27 steals.

Jeter dislocated his shoulder on Opening Day in 2003 and missed 36 games. He finished third in the AL in batting, finishing with 25 doubles, 3 triples, 10 home runs, 52 RBIs and 11 steals. He hit .300 in 17 playoff games with two home runs and five RBIs. In 2006 Jeter hit .343 with 118 runs, 214 hits, 39 doubles, 3 triples, 14 home runs, 97 RBIs and a career-best 34 steals.

In 2009 he hit .334 with 212 hits, 107 runs, 27 doubles, one triple, 18 home runs, 66 RBIs and 30 steals. In 2010 Jeter hit just .270 with 111 runs, 179 hits, 30 doubles, 3 triples, 10 home runs, 67 RBIs and 18 steals on the season. He hit .297 in 2011 with 84 runs, 162 hits, 24 doubles, four triples, six homers, 61 RBIs and 16 steals.

In 2012 Jeter hit .316 while leading the AL in at-bats (683) and hits (216) while scoring 99 runs. He slammed 32 doubles, 15 homers and drove in 58. Jeter hit .333 with two RBIs in the postseason, but he fractured his ankle in Game One of the ALCS and was done for the year. In 2013 he played in just 17 games, hitting .190 with one homer and 7 RBIs.

He announced on Facebook on February 12, 2014, that the 2014 season was his final one in the major leagues. Jeter played 145 games, hitting .256 with four home runs and 50 runs batted in. In his career Jeter played in 2,747 regular season games, scoring 1,923 runs with 3,465 hits; he hit 544 doubles, 66 triples, 260 home runs and drove in 1,311 runs while stealing 358 bases. He posted a career batting average of .310 and had eight 200-hit seasons. In the playoffs, Jeter played in 158 postseason games, helping the Yankees to five World Series championships.

In addition to 14 All-Star Games, Jeter picked up five Gold Glove Awards, five Silver Slugger Awards, two Hank Aaron Awards and a Roberto Clemente Award.

Derek Jeter #2 of the New York Yankees acknowledges the crowd after hitting a single for his last career at bat in the third inning against the Boston Red Sox during the last game of the season at Fenway Park on September 28, 2014 in Boston, MA.

PLAYER STATISTICS:

Position: Shortstop
Born: June 26, 1974
Batted: Right Threw: Right
Hits: 3,465
AVG: .310
HR: 260

TEAMS:
New York Yankees (1995-2014)

HIGHLIGHTS/AWARDS:

- AL Rookie of the Year (1996)
- All-Star MVP (2000)
- AL Babe Ruth Award (2000)
- World Series MVP (2000)
- 2x AL Hank Aaron Award (2006, 2009)
- Roberto Clemente Award (2009)
- Lou Gehrig Memorial Award (2010)
- 5x AL Silver Slugger Award (2006, 2007, 2008, 2009, 2012)
- 5x AL Gold Glove Award (2004, 2005, 2006, 2009, 2010)
- 14x All-Star (1998-2002; 2004; 2006-2012; 2014)

BASEBALL GREATS
WALTER JOHNSON

Known as "The Big Train," Walter Johnson was a power pitcher in an era where it was an anomaly. He boasted a fastball that was roughly estimated to be in the low 90s, nearly unheard of in the early part of the twentieth century. His longevity, consistency and that fastball are all major reasons why he recorded the second-most victories in Major League Baseball.

Johnson played his entire 21-year career with the Washington Senators, who were anything but a powerhouse in the AL during that time. He made his major league debut on August 2, 1907, for a moribund Senators team against the high-flying Detroit Tigers. While Johnson may not have gotten the win in a 3-2 defeat, he made his impact known. Ty Cobb stated that Johnson's arm was the most powerful one he had seen in a major league park at that point in his career.

Unlike most pitchers of the era who used a straight overhand delivery with a windup over their heads, Johnson was a sidearm pitcher. This made it extremely difficult to pick up the ball and made hitting against him challenging. While the Nationals were doormats in the early part of his career, Johnson was a force to be reckoned with. Over his career, he led the league in strikeouts a staggering 12 times, including eight straight seasons from 1912 through 1919.

Johnson would lead the league in victories six times, including four straight seasons from 1913 to 1916. Five times he led the league in ERA, including a 1.14 mark in 1913 that stood as the lowest ERA for a pitcher that threw at least 300 innings in a season until Bob Gibson of the Cardinals broke the mark with a 1.12 ERA in 1968. Johnson led the league in complete games six times, shutouts seven times and WHIP six different times. In a nine-season span between 1910 and 1918, Johnson never threw fewer than 322.1 innings in a season, with a high of 370 frames in 1910. That season, he was 25-17 with a 1.36 ERA, 38 complete games, eight shutouts and 313 strikeouts.

During his pitching career, Johnson won at least 20 games on 12 different occasions, including a stretch of 10 straight seasons between 1910 and 1919. He won more than 30 games twice, going 33-12 with a league-leading 1.39 ERA in 1912 and 36-7 with the aforementioned 1.14 ERA in 1913. He still owns the major league record for career shutouts with 110, a number that likely will never be broken. When he retired in 1927, Johnson owned the major league record for strikeouts in a career with no one even remotely close; Cy Young was next in line with 705 fewer strikeouts.

Johnson was the AL MVP twice, in 1913 and again in 1924. The Senators won two AL pennants during his career, both coming near the end of his tenure. In 1924 Johnson was defeated in Games One and Five by the Giants, but he came on in relief in the ninth inning of Game Seven and threw four scoreless frames. The Senators won the game and the World Series, the only championship of Johnson's career. The next season, Johnson pitched the Senators to a 3-1 series lead against the Pittsburgh Pirates, but he dropped Game Seven with a 9-7 loss, giving up three runs in the eighth inning to deny Washington the World Series title.

When Johnson retired after the 1927 season, he left behind a legacy. He pitched in 802 games, starting 666 of them, and he posted a 417-299 record with a 2.17 career ERA. Johnson pitched 5914.1 innings, allowing 4913 hits, walking 1363 hitters while striking out 3508 with 110 shutouts. His strikeout record held until 1983, and he is still ninth all-time in that category. Johnson is third all-time in innings pitched and 13th in games started; he is also second all-time in victories behind Cy Young. They are the only two major league pitchers to win at least 400 games.

After retiring, Johnson managed the Senators from 1929 through 1932 and the Indians between 1933 and 1935. He was part of the first class inducted into the Baseball Hall of Fame in 1936. He died on December 10, 1946, of a brain tumor at the age of 59.

Walter Johnson poses for a photographer in Washington before a game in 1924.

PLAYER STATISTICS:
Position: Pitcher
Born: November 6, 1887
Died: December 10, 1946 (aged 59)
Batted: Right
Threw: Right
Win-Loss: 417-279
E.R.A. 2.17
SO: 3509 (9th all-time)
ShO: 110
TEAMS:
Washington Senators Player (1907-1927)
Manager (1929-1932)
Cleveland Indians Player (1933-1935)
HIGHLIGHTS/AWARDS:
• 2x MVP Award (1913,1924)
NOTEWORTHY:
• An inaugural member of the National Baseball Hall of Fame: Elected 1936 (Vote 83.63%)
• Played in two World Series (1924, 1925)
• 417 career wins (2nd all-time)
• Pitched 56 consecutive scoreless innings, a record that stood until 1968
• He was named #60 on ESPN's top 100 athletes of the century

BASEBALL GREATS

SANDY KOUFAX

There may not have been a more dominant power pitcher during the 1950s and 1960s as Sandy Koufax. His blazing fastball and effective wildness made him extremely difficult to hit. His six-year run from 1961 through 1966 was one of the most productive stints in the modern era, and had he not been derailed by arthritis in his pitching elbow at the age of 30, there is no telling how his numbers may have ended up.

Koufax had tryouts with the New York Giants and the Pittsburgh Pirates before signing a deal with the Dodgers. After a tryout at Ebbets Field, the Dodgers signed Koufax to a contract with a salary of $6,000 per season and a $14,000 signing bonus. Since his bonus was more than $4,000, league rules at the time stated that he was a "bonus baby" and the Dodgers could not option him to the minors for two years.

Koufax made his major league debut on June 24, 1955, in a game against the Milwaukee Braves. Brooklyn trailed 7-1 in the fifth inning when Koufax came in, and his appearance was less than stellar: he allowed a single, committed an error, walked Hank Aaron and then struck out Bobby Thomson. His first major league victory came in his second start on August 27, 1955, when he blanked the Cincinnati Reds on two hits in a 7-0 Dodgers win.

Still, Koufax was wild and erratic in the first half of his career, and his inconsistency caused the team to have little confidence in him. Koufax never won more than 11 games or threw more than 175 innings in any of his first six seasons. Following the end of the 1960 season, Koufax was convinced he was going to retire, going as far as throwing his glove and spikes into the garbage. He had asked for a trade early in 1960 to get more consistent playing time, but such a deal never materialized.

In 1961 Koufax decided to give baseball one more try. During spring training, Dodgers scout Kenny Myers noticed that when Koufax wound up, he obstructed his own view of home plate. Koufax worked on his delivery and it paid off. He went 18-13 with a 3.52 ERA along with 15 complete games, striking out 269 while walking just 96 hitters. The 269 strikeouts was a new NL record, breaking the mark set by Christy Mathewson back in 1903. He made his first two All-Star Game appearances that season, and suddenly Koufax had turned the corner.

The following year, he became even more dominant. He threw his first no-hitter, turning the trick on the woeful expansion New York Mets on June 30. The Dodgers moved from the Los Angeles Coliseum to the much more pitcher-friendly Dodger Stadium, and Koufax responded by knocking his ERA at home down from 4.29 to 1.75 on the season. Koufax missed significant time with a crushed artery in his palm. He finished the year 14-7 with a league-best 2.54 ERA, but was ineffective after returning from the injury as the Giants caught the Dodgers and eventually bested them in a three-game playoff to claim the NL pennant. The 1962 season would be the first of five consecutive ERA titles for Koufax to close his career.

Koufax's final four seasons in the majors were nothing short of scintillating. He won at least 25 games in three of the seasons and posted a mark of 97-27 in all four seasons, with 89 complete games and 31 shutouts. Three times he broke the 300 strikeout barrier, including a mind-blowing 382 strikeouts in 1965. In 1963, 1965 and 1966 he won the pitching version of the Triple Crown, leading the league in wins, ERA and strikeouts. He won the Cy Young Award in those three seasons at a time when there was only one award for both leagues.

Koufax was forced to retire following the 1966 season due to traumatic arthritis. He finished his career with a record of 165-87 with a 2.76 ERA, 137 complete games, 40 shutouts, and 2,396 strikeouts. He was the NL MVP in 1963 and was the first big league pitcher to toss four no-hitters in his career. He was inducted into the Baseball Hall of Fame in 1972 and at 36 years and 20 days of age is the youngest inductee in history.

Sandy Koufax of the Los Angeles Dodgers winds up a pitch during the first game of the 1963 World Series against the New York Yankees at Yankee Stadium, New York City. The Dodgers won the game and went on to win the series.

PLAYER STATISTICS:

Position: Pitcher
Born: December 30, 1935
Batted: Right
Threw: Left
Win-Loss 165-87
ERA: 2.76
SO: 2396

TEAMS:

Brooklyn/Los Angeles Dodgers (1955–1966)

HIGHLIGHTS/AWARDS:

- Perfect game (1965)
- 2x World Series MVP (1963, 1965)
- NL MVP Award (1963)
- 3x Cy Young Award (1963, 1965, 1966)

NOTEWORTHY:

- Member of the National Baseball Hall of Fame: Elected 1972 (Vote 86.87%, first ballot)
- 7x All-Star
- Second in career no-hitters (4)
- Set single-season record with 382 strikeouts (now is 2nd behind Nolan Ryan's 383 in 1973)
- Holds single-season record for most shutouts by a left-handed pitcher (11), breaking previous record (9) set by Babe Ruth in 1916
- Led National League in ERA 5 years in a row
- Led National League in strikeouts 4 times
- Led National League in shutouts 3 times
- Led National League in wins 3 times
- 0.95 ERA in 4 World Series

BASEBALL GREATS

MICKEY MANTLE

The New York Yankees are well known for having some of the greatest and most famous players in Major League Baseball. One of these players is Mickey Mantle, who spent his entire 18-year big league career with the team. He began his career as a right fielder but would take over the center field post that fellow Hall of Famer DiMaggio had patrolled during his career.

The Yankees signed Mantle as an amateur free agent in 1949 and he played for the Class D Independence Yankees of the Kansas-Oklahoma-Missouri League. He was promoted to the Joplin Miners of the Class C's Western Association in 1950 and responded by winning the league's batting title, hitting .383 with 26 home runs and 136 RBIs.

Mantle had a terrific spring training in 1951 with the major league club and manager Casey Stengel decided to keep him up with the big club. Mantle originally wore number six and made his major league debut on April 17, 1951, as a right fielder, going 1-for-4 with a run scored and a run batted in for the Yankees, who beat Boston 5-0 that day.

Mantle suffered a slump and the Yankees sent him down to their Triple A affiliate, the Kansas City Blues. He hit .361 with 11 home runs and 50 RBIs for the Blues before being recalled. He finished his rookie season hitting .267 with 13 home runs and 65 RBIs over the course of 96 games. He played just two games in the World Series that year, which the Yankees won in six games.

In 1952 Mantle moved to center field, replacing the retired DiMaggio and responding with a .311 average, 23 home runs and 87 RBIs over 142 games. He was more productive in the World Series than he was in 1951, having 10 hits, including a pair of home runs, as the Yankees defeated the Brooklyn Dodgers in seven games to repeat as champions. Mantle would drive in 100 runs for the first time in his career in 1954, when he drove in 102. He also led the league in runs-scored that season with 129.

Mantle led the league in home runs for the first time in 1955 when he hit 37 and also led in triples with 11. He enjoyed his finest year in 1956, winning the AL Triple Crown with a .353 average, 52 home runs and 130 RBIs. He was also the leader in runs scored (132), slugging percentage (.705), OPS (1.169) and total bases (376). For his efforts, he won his very first AL MVP Award.

Mantle would repeat as the AL MVP in 1957, hitting a career-best .365 which was second to Ted Williams' .388 mark, along with 34 home runs and 94 RBIs; Mantle did lead the league in runs scored (121) and walks (146), however. In 1958 for the third consecutive season, he led in runs scored (127) and also in home runs (42), walks (129), strikeouts (120), total bases (307) and intentional walks (13). He finished second in the MVP voting in 1960 and 1961.

Mantle claimed his third and final MVP Award in 1962 when he finished the year with a .321 average along with 30 home runs and 89 RBIs over 121 games. He also led the league in walks (122), on-base percentage (.486), slugging percentage (.605) and OPS (1.091) while winning the only Gold Glove of his career. It was the last best season he had as he struggled with injuries and declining statistics in his final years. From 1963 to 1968, just once did he hit more than 23 home runs and drive in more than 56 runs.

In 1967 Mantle moved to first base and after back-to-back subpar seasons, he had a tough decision to make. He announced his retirement on March 1, 1969, and retired having played in 2,401 games and posting a .298 career batting average, 536 home runs, 1509 RBIs, three MVP Awards, a Gold Glove, seven World Series championships and 20 All-Star appearances.

Mantle was inducted to the Baseball Hall of Fame in 1974, his first year of eligibility. The Yankees retired his number seven on June 8, 1969, which was "Mickey Mantle Day" at Yankee Stadium. He died on August 13, 1995, at the age of 64 from liver cancer.

Mickey Mantle poses for the camera with bat in hand in this undated photo.

PLAYER STATISTICS:

Position: Center fielder
Born: October 20, 1931
Died: August 13, 1995 (aged 63)
Batted: Switch
Threw: Right
Hits: 2415
AVG: .298
HR: 536

TEAMS:

New York Yankees (1951-1968)

HIGHLIGHTS/AWARDS:

- 3x AL MVP (1956, 1957, & 1962)
- AL Triple Crown (1956)
- AL Gold Glove (1962)

NOTEWORTHY:

- 20x AL All-Star (1952-1965, 1967, 1968)
- Member of the National Baseball Hall of Fame: Elected 1974 (Vote 88.2%, first ballot)
- Led league in batting average (1956)
- Led league in home runs (1955, 1956, 1958, & 1960)
- Led league in RBIs (1956)

BASEBALL GREATS

CHRISTY MATHEWSON

The only pitcher to be ranked in the top ten all-time for victories and ERA, Christy Mathewson had less than a stellar start to his big league career before settling in as one of the most dominant pitchers of the dead ball era.

Mathewson spent all but one game of his major league career pitching for the New York Giants. He started off sluggishly, going 0-3 with a 5.08 ERA in six games, one start, in the 1900 season. He issued more walks (20) than he had strikeouts (15) over 33.2 innings, and was sent back to the minors to work on his control. The Cincinnati Reds picked him up, but they dealt him back to the Giants on December 15.

He was back with the team for the 1901 season and pitched in 40 games, starting 38. He went 20-17 with a 2.41 ERA with 36 games and five shutouts over 336 innings. While he walked 97 hitters and threw a league-leading 23 wild pitches, Mathewson struck out 221 hitters and quickly became one of the elite pitchers in the NL. He helped lead the Giants to the 1904 NL pennant, as he went 33-12 with a 2.03 ERA while starting a league-high 46 games and recording a league-best 212 strikeouts.

He was terrific in 1905, winning the pitching Triple Crown with 31 wins, a 1.28 ERA and 206 strikeouts. In the 1905 World Series, Mathewson threw three complete game shutouts to lead the Giants to a five-game victory over the Philadelphia A's. He won a second pitching Triple Crown in 1908 in a season that saw him post a 37-11 mark with a 1.43 ERA and 259 strikeouts. He also led the league in games pitched (56), games started (44), complete games (34), shutouts (11) and saves (5), and he impressively walked just 42 hitters on the season. The Giants fell a game behind the Cubs in the NL standings, mainly due to "Merkle's Boner," where Fred Merkle forgot to touch second base on a potential game-winning hit. The game was called on account of darkness and was made up at the end of the season with the Cubs and Giants tied with 98-55 records. On October 8, 1908, Mathewson gamely took the mound with a sore arm but gave up four runs as Mordecai "Three Finger" Brown pitched Chicago to a 4-2 win.

Mathewson excelled for the next five seasons, winning at least 23 games in each from 1909 to 1913. He led the Giants to three straight pennants between 1911 and 1913, but New York fell in the World Series each time. The Giants were defeated by the A's in 1911, by the Red Sox in 1912, and then Philadelphia bested them in 1913. By this point, Mathewson's best seasons were in the rear-view mirror.

In 1914 Mathewson posted a 24-13 mark for the Giants with a 3.00 ERA, but he allowed a league-high 16 home runs en route to giving up 133 runs (104 earned) in 312 innings of work. He was more hittable, as he fanned just 80 hitters on the season while walking a mere 23. The Giants finished second in the NL with an 84-70 mark. By 1915, Mathewson had slumped to an 8-14 mark with a 3.58 ERA in 27 games, 24 starts as the Giants sunk to the basement of the NL.

On July 20, 1916, Mathewson was traded to the Cincinnati Reds. He signed a three-year deal to be the team's manager but pitched in just one game for the Reds. In the second game of a doubleheader against the Cubs on September 4, 1916, Mathewson pitched a complete game victory in a 10-8 triumph over Chicago and his old nemesis, Brown. It would prove to be his last outing as a major league pitcher; he retired at the end of the season.

Mathewson pitched in 636 games, starting 552 of them. He posted a record of 373-188 with a 2.13 ERA over 4788.2 innings, allowing 4219 hits and walking 848 hitters while striking out 2507. He is tied with Grover Cleveland Alexander for the most wins by a NL pitcher with 373 and was enshrined in the Baseball Hall of Fame in 1936. He died on October 7, 1925, at the age of 45 from tuberculosis that he developed as a result of an accidental gassing during a training exercise as a member of the United States Army during World War I.

Christy Mathewson works out for the New York Giants in the Polo Grounds in 1907.

PLAYER STATISTICS:

Position:	Pitcher
Born:	August 12, 1880
Died:	October 7, 1925 (aged 45)
Batted:	Right Threw: Right
Win-Loss:	Record 373-188
ERA:	2.13
SO:	2502
ShO:	79 (3rd all time)

TEAMS:

New York Giants	Player (1900-1916)
Cincinnati Reds	Player (1916)
	Manager (1916-1918)

HIGHLIGHTS/AWARDS:

- Won NL Pitcher's Triple Crown (1905, 1908)
- Five-time ERA champion (1905, 1908, 1909, 1911, 1913)
- Five-time strikeout champion (1903, 1904, 1905, 1907, 1908)

NOTEWORTHY:

- Member of the National Baseball Hall of Fame: Elected 1936 (Vote 90.7%, first ballot)
- 373 career wins (3rd all-time)
- 2.13 career ERA (8th all-time)
- 1.059 career WHIP (5th all time)
- Won 20 games or more 13 times,
- Won 30 games or more 4 times.

BASEBALL GREATS

WILLIE MAYS

One of the greatest defensive center fielders in Major League Baseball history, Willie Mays made spectacular plays look routine. Over the course of his 22-year career, he was as complete a five-tool player that baseball had to offer. He could hit for power (660 career home runs, fourth all time), run (338 career steals), field (12 Gold Glove Awards) and throw (195 outfield assists, 60 double plays).

Mays began his career with the Chattanooga Choo-Choos in the Negro League in 1947, and then returned to his home state of Alabama to play for the Birmingham Black Barons. He had tryouts with the Boston Braves and Brooklyn Dodgers, but both teams passed. Acting on a tip, the Giants signed him in 1950 and sent him to the minors.

On May 25, 1951, Mays made his major league debut against the Philadelphia Phillies. He batted third and played center field in an 8-5 Giants victory, going 0-for-5 with a strikeout. He started his career 0-for-12 before homering off Warren Spahn at the Polo Grounds. Mays finished his rookie season hitting .274 with 20 home runs and 68 RBIs over the course of 121 games. Claiming the Rookie of the Year Award that season, he was in the on-deck circle when Bobby Thomson hit his famous "Shot Heard Round the World" that gave the Giants the NL pennant. Mays missed most of the 1952 and 1953 seasons after being drafted during the Korean War.

Mays returned in 1954 as if he missed no time at all. He won the NL MVP Award after leading the league with a .345 average to go with 41 home runs and 110 RBIs. He also led in triples with 13 and made his first of 24 appearances in the All-Star Game. Mays saved his best and most well-known play for the postseason. In Game One of the World Series against the Cleveland Indians, the score was tied in the eighth inning, though Cleveland had runners on first and second with no outs. The Giants went to reliever Don Liddle to face the left-handed-hitting Vic Wertz. Wertz worked the count to two balls and one strike, crushing a Liddle offering to deep center field some 420 feet from home plate. In most ballparks, this would be a home run, but in the cavernous Polo Grounds it was playable. Mays made an outstanding over-the-shoulder catch that prevented any runs from scoring. Mays scored the winning run in the 10th inning and the floored Indians never recovered, swept aside in four straight games. It would be the only World Series championship for Mays in his prolific career.

In 1957 Mays became just the second major leaguer to hit 20 doubles, 20 triples, 20 home runs and steal 20 bases in the same year when he had 26 doubles, 20 triples, 35 home runs and a league-leading 38 steals. He is also the only player to hit three triples in one game and four home runs in another. Mays led the league in home runs four times, with a career-high 52 blasts coming in 1965. He also led the league in triples three times, steals four times, runs-scored twice and total bases on three occasions. He was MVP twice, first in 1954, and then again in 1965.

The Giants traded Mays to the Mets in May of 1972. The Giants were losing money, and ownership could not promise him any income after he retired; the Mets offered him a job as a coach once he hung up his cleats. Mays would play 133 games in a Mets uniform, making his final postseason appearance as the Mets lost the 1973 World Series in seven games to the Oakland A's. Mays hit his 660th and final home run on August 17 against Cincinnati's Don Gullett and retired after the season.

Mays finished his career with a .302 batting average, 660 home runs, 1,903 RBIs, 338 stolen bases, a dozen consecutive Gold Gloves and 2,992 games. He still holds the major league record for extra-inning home runs with 22, and he is the only player in major league history to have hit a home run in every inning from the first through the sixteenth during his career. Mays was inducted as a first-ballot Hall of Famer in 1979, being named on 94.7 percent of the ballots.

Willie Mays, wearing his San Francisco Giants uniform and flip-up sunglasses, taking a break during a training session.

PLAYER STATISTICS:

Position:	Center fielder
Born:	May 6, 1931
Batted:	Right
Threw:	Right
AVG:	.302
HR:	660 (4th overall)
Hits:	3,283
TB:	6,066 (3rd overall)

TEAMS:

New York/San Francisco Giants (1951-1952, 1954-1972)
New York Mets (1972-1973)

HIGHLIGHTS/AWARDS:

- 24x All-Star
- 2x NL MVP (1954, 1965)
- 12x NL Gold Glove Award (1957-1968)

NOTEWORTHY:

- Member of the National Baseball Hall of Fame: Elected 1979 (Vote 94.7%, first ballot)
- 1st player with 500 home runs and 3,000 hits

BASEBALL GREATS

STAN MUSIAL

Stan Musial embodied the epitome of the difference between sports in his era and sports in the current era. Musial played his entire 22-season career with the St. Louis Cardinals. In the era of free agency and multimillion dollar contracts, the chance of seeing a star player start and finish his career with the same team is slim. One can only speculate what a player with Musial's credentials would make in this day and age.

Musial was signed as an amateur free agent by the Cardinals before the 1938 season. He was signed as a pitcher, but converted to an outfielder before making his major league debut. His first big league appearance came on September 17, 1941. That day, Musial was 2-for-4 with a single, double and two RBIs as the Cardinals bested the Boston Braves, 3-2. He would play 12 games for the Cardinals in 1941, going 20 of 47 (.426) with four doubles, one home run and seven RBIs.

Musial played in his first World Series in 1942. He hit .315 with 10 home runs and 72 RBIs for the Cardinals, while playing both corner outfield positions. The next season, in 1943, he won his first MVP Award after leading the NL in several offensive categories: games played (157), plate appearances (700), hits (220), doubles (48), triples (20), batting average (.357), on-base percentage (.425), slugging percentage (.562) and OPS (.988). All that success failed to deliver a repeat championship, as the Yankees beat St. Louis in five games.

Musial claimed his second World Series championship in 1944 as the Cardinals defeated the St. Louis Browns in six games. For the regular season, Musial hit .347 with a league-leading 197 hits along with 51 doubles, 12 home runs and 94 RBIs. He missed the 1945 season after entering the United States Navy on January 23, 1945, and spent nearly 14 months in the military before being discharged in March 1946.

Musial returned to the baseball scene with a vengeance in 1946. He claimed his second MVP Award after leading the league in games (156), plate appearances (702), at-bats (624), hits (228), runs scored (124), doubles (50), triples (20), batting average (.365), slugging percentage (.587), OPS (1.021) and total bases (366); those numbers allowed him to easily outdistance Brooklyn's Dixie Walker to claim the award. St. Louis won their third championship with Musial, defeating the Red Sox in seven games. Musial struggled with appendicitis and tonsillitis in 1947, but refused to have either his appendix or his tonsils removed until after the season.

The 1948 season saw Musial claim his third MVP Award, making him the first NL player to win three MVP Awards in a career. He continued his hitting prowess into the 1950s, claiming batting titles in 1950, 1951, 1952 and 1957. He led the league in runs scored in 1951, 1952 and 1954, and in hits in 1952. Musial also led in doubles three straight years from 1952 to 1954, in triples in 1951, in RBIs during the 1956 season, and in on-base percentage in 1953 and 1957. He finished second in the MVP voting in 1949, 1950, 1951 and 1957, while making the All-Star Game every year from 1943 through 1963.

Musial played his final game on September 29, 1963. The Cardinals retired his number six on the spot, and just as Musial had two hits in his major league debut, he had two hits in the final game of his career. He was lifted for a pinch-runner after singling home Curt Flood in the sixth inning. Musial finished his career with 3,630 hits and, in a statistical anomaly, they were evenly split: 1,815 hits at home and 1,815 of them on the road. His career average was a stellar .331, to go along with 475 home runs and 1951 RBIs. He was enshrined in the Baseball Hall of Fame in his first year of eligibility in 1969.

On February 11, 2011, Musial was awarded the Presidential Medal of Freedom by President Barack Obama. Musial passed away on January 19, 2013, at the age of 92. A memorial wreath was laid at the base of the statue bearing his likeness at Busch Stadium.

Stan Musial watches the ball as he follows through after a hit during a game circa 1955. Musial wears the uniform of the St. Louis Cardinals, his team for the entire length of his professional career (1941 to 1963).

PLAYER STATISTICS:

Position:	Outfielder / First baseman
Born:	November 21, 1920
Died:	January 9, 2013 (aged 92)
Batted:	Left
Threw:	Left
AVG:	.331
Hits:	3,630
HR	475
RBI	1,951

TEAMS

St. Louis Cardinals (1941–1944, 1946–1963)

HIGHLIGHTS/AWARDS:

- 24x All-Star
- 3x World Series champion (1942, 1944, 1946)
- 3x NL MVP (1943, 1946, 1948)
- 7x NL batting title (1943, 1946, 1948, 1950, 1951, 1952, 1957)
- 1957 Lou Gehrig Memorial Award

NOTEWORTHY:

- St. Louis Cardinals #6 retired
- Member of the National Baseball Hall of Fame Induction 1969 Vote 93.2% (first ballot)
- Major League Baseball All-Century Team

BASEBALL GREATS

CAL RIPKEN JR.

To say that Cal Ripken Jr. was a throwback player may be the ultimate compliment. He played for the Baltimore Orioles his entire career, which spanned 21 seasons from 1981 through 2001. Ripken made history on September 6, 1995, when he played in his 2,131st consecutive game to break Lou Gehrig's ironman record. Ripken would tack another 501 on before he was finished.

Ripken was selected by the Orioles in the second round of the 1978 MLB amateur draft. He made his major league debut on August 10, 1981, scoring the winning run in the 12th inning of a 3-2 game over Kansas City as a pinch-runner. He had just five hits in 39 at-bats that season, finishing with a .128 average. He claimed the AL Rookie of the Year Award in 1982 while splitting time between third base and shortstop, hitting .264 with 28 home runs and 93 RBIs.

The next year Ripken was even better, winning the AL MVP Award in just his second full year in the majors. He led the league in games played (162), plate appearances (726), at-bats (663), runs scored (121), hits (211) and doubles (47), while slamming 27 home runs and driving in 102 with a .318 batting average. The Orioles won the 1983 World Series, knocking off the Philadelphia Phillies in five games.

Ripken hit at least 20 home runs in 10 consecutive seasons from 1982 through 1991, and until he was taken out in a blowout loss to the Toronto Blue Jays on September 14, 1987, he had played 8,243 consecutive innings. Ripken won his second MVP Award in 1991 when he led the AL in total bases with 368. He had 210 hits, including 47 doubles, along with a .323 batting average and career-best totals in home runs (34) and RBIs (114.) He also claimed the Gold Glove and Silver Slugger Awards and was the All-Star Game MVP; he went 2-for-3 with a three-run home run off Dennis Martinez and claimed the All-Star Game Home Run Derby. Ripken became the first AL MVP to win the award while playing on a team with a losing record as the Orioles were a dismal 67-95.

He had his 2,000th career hit in 1993, but the big moment came on September 6, 1995, when he broke Gehrig's record for consecutive games played in front of a capacity crowd at Camden Yards against the Angels. After the top of the fifth inning when the game was official, he was the recipient of one of the longest standing ovations ever for an athlete, lasting well over 20 minutes. On June 14, 1996, he shattered the world record for consecutive games by playing in his 2,216th game in a row; it had been held previously by Japan's Sachio Kinugasa, who played for the Hiroshima Carp.

Ripken played with the Orioles through the 2001 season. His consecutive games streak came to a halt on his own terms after his 2,632nd game on September 20, 1998. He battled through injuries at the beginning and end of the 1999 season, and he also had to deal with the death of his father. Ripken picked up his 3,000th hit on April 15, 2000.

The 2001 season was Ripken's last, and he played in the All-Star Game one last time. Alex Rodriguez changed positions with Ripken, letting Ripken play shortstop as he had for the majority of his career instead of third base. In his first at-bat in the game, Ripken homered off Chan Ho Park and was awarded the All-Star Game MVP for the second time. Ripken is one of four players with multiple All-Star Game MVP Awards and the only one to win them in different decades. The Orioles retired his number eight prior to his final game.

Ripken appeared in 3001 games, finishing with a .276 career average, 431 home runs and 1,695 RBIs. He was named to 19 All-Star Games, claimed eight Silver Slugger Awards, two Gold Glove Awards, two AL MVPs, two All-Star Game MVPs, the AL Rookie of the Year, and he played on a World Series winning team. He was inducted into the Baseball Hall of Fame in 2007, his first year of eligibility. He was named on 98.53 percent of the ballots, the third-highest percentage of all time, trailing only Tom Seaver and Nolan Ryan.

National League third baseman Chipper Jones (L) of the Atlanta Braves gets to third safely past the tag of American League third baseman Cal Ripken, Jr.(R) of the Baltimore Orioles during play of the 1998 Major League All-Star game at Coors Field in Denver, CO.

PLAYER STATISTICS:

Position: Shortstop/Third Base
Born: August 24, 1960
Batted: Right
Threw: Right
Hits: 3184
AVG: .276
HR: 431

TEAMS

Baltimore Orioles (1981-2001)

HIGHLIGHTS/AWARDS:

- 19x MLB All-Star 1983-2001 (DNP 2000)
- 2x MLB All-Star Game MVP (1991, 2001)
- AL Rookie of the Year (1982)
- 2x AL MVP (1983, 1991)
- 2x AL Gold Glove Award (1991, 1992)
- 8x AL Silver Slugger Award (1983-86, 1989, 1991, 1993-94)

NOTEWORTHY:

- Member of the National Baseball Hall of Fame Elected 2007 (Vote 98.53%)
- Most Consecutive Games Played: 2,632
- MLB All-Century Team

BASEBALL GREATS

JACKIE ROBINSON

Jack Roosevelt Robinson helped end 80 years of baseball segregation when he became the first African American Major League Baseball player of the modern era, making his debut with the Brooklyn Dodgers in 1947. Born on January 31, 1919, in Cairo, Georgia, Robinson was brought up surrounded by poverty and during an era where racial prejudice against African Americans was rife. Despite the hardships Robinson faced, he went on to become one of baseball's finest-ever players, not only as a disciplined hitter but also as a versatile fielder and successful second baseman.

Robinson's professional career first started in 1945 when he joined the Negro League Kansas City Monarchs. In late 1945, Branch Rickey, the club president and general manager of the Brooklyn Dodgers, made the unprecedented move to assign Robinson for the 1946 season to the Montreal Royals, a minor league affiliate of the Brooklyn Dodgers. His performance with the Royals earned Robinson a spot with the Dodgers in the 1947 major league season and on April 15 of that year played in his first game with the Brooklyn Dodgers, marking the first time in 57 years that racial prejudice, otherwise known as the baseball "color line," had been broken in the major leagues.

During the early years of his major league career, both players and fans alike taunted Robinson with severe and indecent racial harassment. However, there were some that welcomed Robinson, including fellow team member Pee Wee Reese and Jewish baseball star Hank Greenberg. The Dodger management also threatened that any player on their roster who continued to harass the rookie would have to find employment elsewhere.

Despite the controversy surrounding him, Robinson went on to play 151 games in his first year, hit .297, led the National League in stolen bases and was awarded the first-ever Rookie of the Year Award. In 1949, Robinson was awarded the National League MVP, with a batting average of .342, 16 home runs and a league-best 37 stolen bases.

In the following seasons, Robinson continued to be an integral player on the Dodgers lineup. In 1955 he helped the team secure the World Series over the New York Yankees. By the end of the 1956 season, however, Robinson was traded to the New York Giants. Rather than play for another team, Robinson chose to retire from Major League Baseball prior to the 1957 season. He finished his 10-season playing career with a .311 batting average and more than double as many walks than strikeouts. He was also an outstanding base stealer, finishing with a career total of 19 steals of home plate—no other player since World War I has surpassed this record. Robinson played in six All-Star Games and six World Series championships.

After his retirement Robinson served on the NAACP board until 1967. In 1962 he became the first African American to be inducted into the Baseball Hall of Fame. In March 1984 he was awarded the Presidential Medal of Freedom by then-US President Ronald Reagan and in 1987 the Rookie of the Year Award was renamed the Jackie Robinson Award in his honor. In 1997 his number 42 was retired by Major League Baseball, and in 1999 he was named by *Time Magazine* on its list of 100 most influential people of the twentieth century. That same year he was ranked number 44 by *The Sporting News* on the list of 100 Greatest Baseball Players of all time and was included in the Major League Baseball All-Century Team as the highest voted second baseman with 788,116 votes.

A portrait of the Brooklyn Dodgers' infielder Jackie Robinson in uniform.

PLAYER STATISTICS:

Position: Second Baseman
Born: January 31, 1919
Died: October 24, 1972 (aged 53)
Batted: Right
Threw: Right
AVG: .311
Hits: 1518
HR: 137

TEAMS:

Brooky Dodgers (1947 - 1956)

HIGHLIGHTS/AWARDS:

- National League R.O.Y. Award (1947)
- 1949 National League MVP Award (1949)
- 6x All-Star
- 1962 Member of the National Baseball Hall of Fame. (vote 77.5%, first ballot)

NOTEWORTHY:

- His #42 was retired from Major League Baseball in 1997 to honour the 50th anniversary of his first Major League game.

BASEBALL GREATS

PETE ROSE

There are few players in the history of professional sports that are as polarizing as Pete Rose. He is loved by some for his hustle and love of the game and despised by others, who claim that his betting on games while managing the Cincinnati Reds was one of the ultimate travesties in a sport that has seen its fair share of questionable events and poor decision-making. Regardless of what one's thoughts are about Rose as an individual, as a player he holds records that may indeed never be broken.

Rose was signed by the Cincinnati Reds as an amateur free agent in 1960, and he would get his chance in the majors during spring training in 1963 when regular starting second baseman Don Blasingame pulled a groin muscle. He would get the nickname Charlie Hustle from Hall of Fame pitcher Whitey Ford, who called Rose that when he ran down to first base after drawing a walk. Rose made the major league team that season.

He made his debut on April 8, 1963, against the Pittsburgh Pirates, going 0-for-3 with a walk, a strikeout and a run-scored in the Reds' 5-2 win over the Pirates. He would get his first big league hit on April 13 when he tripled off Pittsburgh's Bob Friend. Rose would finish the season with a .273 batting average, 101 runs scored, six home runs and 41 RBIs. He won the NL Rookie of the Year Award for his performance, garnering 17 of 20 first place votes.

Rose earned his first All-Star nod in 1965 as he led the league in plate appearances (757), at-bats (670) and hits (209), while hitting .312 with 11 home runs and 81 RBIs. It was the first of 17 All-Star appearances for Rose, who would set a record for being selected as an All-Star at five different positions: second base, left field, right field, third base and first base. That was also the first of nine consecutive seasons that saw Rose hit over .300 through 1973.

Rose led the league in hits in 1968 with 210, and also in average as he claimed his first batting title with a .335 average. He also led the league in on-base percentage with a .391 mark and finished second in the NL MVP Award voting behind St. Louis's Bob Gibson, who posted a 1.12 ERA in the "Year of the Pitcher." Rose led the league in hitting again in 1969 with a .348 average and scored a league-best 120 runs. He hit a career-best 16 home runs that season and won his first Gold Glove.

Rose claimed the only MVP of his career in 1973 as he led the league in plate appearances (752), at-bats (680), hits (230) and batting average for the third time in his career with a .338 mark. Rose led the league in runs scored and doubles in 1974, 1975 and 1976. He also led the league in hits in 1976 with 215, marking the sixth time in his career to that point that he had led the league in that category. After the 1978 season, in which Rose hit .302 with a league-best 51 doubles, 7 home runs and 52 RBIs, the Reds declined to offer him a new deal, allowing him to become a free agent.

The Philadelphia Phillies made Rose the highest-paid player in team sports at the time when they signed him to a four-year deal worth $3.2 million. He would help the Phillies win their first World Series championship in 1980, and led the league in hits for the final time in his career in the strike-shortened season of 1981 at the age of 40. He led the league in on-base percentage and had his final 200-hit season in 1980 when he banged out 208 hits.

Rose's final season with Philadelphia in 1983 was the worst of his career, and he hit just .245 with just 14 doubles and no home runs. He was benched for stretches during the latter part of the season, though he played better in the playoffs. Despite that late-season resurgence, the Phillies lost in the World Series to the Baltimore Orioles. Rose complained about his benching during a World Series interview with Howard Cosell of ABC Sports, which would help cement his demise in Philadelphia.

Pete Rose #14 of the Philadelphia Phillies swings at a pitch during a game in the 1980s.

PLAYER STATISTICS:

Position:	Outfielder / Infielder / Manager
Born:	April 14, 1941 (age 73)
Batted:	Switch
Threw:	Right
AVG:	.303
Hits:	4,256 (MLB record)
HR:	160
RBI:	314
G:	3,562 (MLB record)
AB:	14,053 (MLB record)

TEAMS:

Cincinnati Reds	Player (1963–1978)
Philadelphia Phillies	Player (1979–1983)
Montreal Expos	Player (1984)
Cincinnati Reds	Player (1984–1986)
	Manager (1984–1989)

HIGHLIGHTS/AWARDS:

- 3x World Series champion (1975, 1976, 1980)
- NL MVP (1973)
- World Series MVP (1975)
- 3x NL Batting Champion (1968, 1969, 1973)
- 17x All-Star
- 2x Gold Glove Award (1969, 1970)
- Silver Slugger Award (1981)
- NL Rookie of the Year (1963)
- Hutch Award (1968)
- Lou Gehrig Memorial Award (1969)
- Roberto Clemente Award (1976)
- Major League Baseball All-Century Team

BASEBALL GREATS

BABE RUTH

It's hard to accurately predict what most people remember Babe Ruth for, as there were so many things that stand out about the slugger. Many will remember him for his prodigious power during an era where home runs were uncommon; others recall his pitching ability before he transitioned to an everyday player. The "called" home run off the Cubs' Charley Root in the 1932 World Series or the "Curse of the Bambino" also are likely to be remembered about the "Sultan of Swat." Ruth began his professional career in 1913 with the Baltimore Orioles, who at the time were a minor league franchise. They made a deal with the Boston Red Sox, and Ruth made his major league debut for the Red Sox on July 11, 1914.

Ruth was a starting pitcher for the majority of his career in Boston. He twice won 20 games in a season, and overall went 89-46 with a 2.19 ERA over the course of six seasons. In 1918 he began to play the outfield with more regularity following a suggestion from teammate Harry Hooper that Ruth's bat in the lineup could be highly beneficial to Boston's chances. Ruth led the league with 11 home runs despite playing in just 95 games; it was the first of 12 home run crowns.

The turning point in Ruth's career was Harry Frazee's move to sell him to the Yankees, who were struggling at the time. After the 1919 season, Ruth demanded a raise to $20,000 a year. Frazee refused to pay the sum and decided to trade Ruth, but was limited to the Chicago White Sox and the Yankees as potential trading partners. Chicago offered $60,000 and Shoeless Joe Jackson, while the Yankees offered $100,000 cash. The deal was finalized with the Yankees, and Frazee received $125,000 and three $25,000 notes that were payable at 6 percent interest yearly in addition to a $300,000 loan with the mortgage on Fenway Park as collateral. On December 26, 1919, the deal was done and baseball history was set to be changed once again. The Red Sox had claimed World Series championships with Ruth in 1915, 1916 and 1918 and would not win again until 2004. Meanwhile, the Yankees became a dominant force, winning four titles in Ruth's tenure with the team.

Ruth, who had broken Ned Williamson's major league record of 27 home runs in his final year in Boston when he hit 29, obliterated his own mark in his first year with the Yankees. He slammed 54 home runs in 1920, more than any other team in the league that year barring the Philadelphia Phillies, who hit 64. The next season, he upped his total to 59 and became the majors' all-time home run leader with his 139th on July 18, 1921. Ruth would hit another 575 home runs in his career to finish with 714, which is still the third-best total all time, trailing only Barry Bonds and Hank Aaron. Ruth is well known for being part of the 1927 "Murderer's Row" Yankees lineup that also featured Lou Gehrig, Bob Meusel, Tony Lazzeri and others. He also is famed for driving a pitch beyond the center field flagpole at Wrigley Field on a 0-2 pitch from Charley Root. The hit, which was part showmanship and part talent, helped the Yankees to a 7-5 victory in Game Three of the 1932 World Series. Ruth's blow sapped Chicago's morale, and the Yankees would blast the Cubs 13-6 in Game Four to complete a sweep.

Ruth was traded to the Boston Braves in 1935. They were swimming in debt and hopeful that Ruth would draw more fans to the stadium to bolster their bottom line, but he was out of shape and barely able to do much other than hit. Once the season wore on, he stopped hitting as well. He hit his final three home runs on May 25, 1935, at Forbes Field against the Pittsburgh Pirates. His 714th and final home run cleared the roof of Forbes Field, making him the first to accomplish the feat. He announced his retirement on May 27, 1935, finishing his career with a .342 average, 714 home runs and 2,213 RBIs. He also drew a staggering 2,062 walks against just 1,330 strikeouts and still holds the major league record with a .690 career slugging percentage.

Babe Ruth takes a big swing during a batting practice session before a game in 1921 at the Polo Grounds in New York City.

PLAYER STATISTICS:

Position: Outfielder/Pitcher
Born: February 6, 1895
Died: August 16, 1948 (aged 53)
Batted: Left
Threw: Left
AVG: .342
HR: 714 (3rd - All Time)
RBI: 2217
Win/Loss: 94-46
ERA: 2.28
Career SLUG: 0.690
Career OPS: 1.164

TEAMS:

Boston Red Sox (1914–1919)
New York Yankees (1920–1934)
Boston Braves (1935)

HIGHLIGHTS/AWARDS:

- Won the 1923 AL League Award (precursor to MVP)
- Appeared in 1933 & 1934 All-Star Game
- First player ever to hit 30, 40, 50 and 60 home runs in a season

NOTEWORTHY:

- Member of the National Baseball Hall of Fame Elected 1936 (Vote 95.13%)
- 2nd in career OBP (.469)
- 3rd on All-Time Home Run list (714)
- Only player to hit 3 home runs twice in a World Series game (1926 & 1928)

BASEBALL GREATS

NOLAN RYAN

When it comes to striking out opposing hitters, no pitcher accomplished the feat more often than Nolan Ryan. "The Ryan Express" would fan a major league-record 5,714 hitters in his career, which leaves him 839 strikeouts ahead of his nearest competitor, Randy Johnson. There is no one else within 1,000 strikeouts of Ryan's total, and it is hard to fathom anyone coming remotely close to breaking his record. He pitched 27 years in the majors and is the only player to have his number retired by three different teams.

Ryan's career began after he was drafted in the 12th round of the 1965 MLB Draft by the New York Mets. He made his major league debut on September 11, 1966, in an 8-3 loss to the Atlanta Braves. Ryan threw two innings in relief of losing pitcher Dennis Ribant, allowing one run on one hit, while walking one and recording his first three strikeouts. Ryan finished 1966 with a mark of 0-1 and a 15.00 ERA, as he gave up four runs on four hits with two walks and three strikeouts in one inning in his first start, a 9-2 loss to Houston on September 18.

Ryan missed most of 1967 with injury, illness and time spent in the Army Reserves, and he didn't make it onto the Mets roster full time until 1968. He remained a spot starter and reliever for most of his tenure with them, helping the team to the 1969 World Series. He saved Game Three of the Series, pitching 2.1 innings against the Orioles to give the Mets a two-games-to-one advantage. They claimed their first championship in five games. After a disappointing 1971 campaign, Ryan was frustrated and contemplating retirement. He approached the Mets about a trade and on December 10, 1971, he was dealt to the California Angels. California gave him his first chance as a consistent starter in 1972, and he responded with a 19-16 record with a 2.28 ERA, 20 complete games and a league-leading nine shutouts. Ryan also fanned an AL-leading 329 batters, and set a major league record allowing just 5.26 hits per nine innings while earning an All-Star berth for the first time.

Ryan posted a pair of 20-win seasons in 1973 and 1974. During his eight years with the team, he led the league in strikeouts seven times, including a major league-record 383 in 1973. Ryan threw four no-hitters in three years: two in 1973 and one each in 1974 and 1975. In his second no-hitter on July 15, 1973, against the Detroit Tigers, Detroit slugger Norm Cash came up to the plate with two outs in the ninth inning carrying a table leg instead of a bat after striking out three times previously in the game. The prank is one of the most well-remembered in baseball history.

Ryan took his arm to Houston, signing a contract with the Astros in 1979. They made the playoffs in 1980 but fell one game short of advancing to the World Series. He threw his league-leading fifth no-hitter in 1981, winning the NL ERA title as he went 11-5 with a 1.69 ERA, helping the Astros to another playoff run. On April 27, 1983, Ryan became Major League Baseball's strikeout king when he fanned Brad Mills for his 3,509th strikeout, besting Walter Johnson's mark.

Ryan left Houston after a contract dispute in 1988 and signed with the Texas Rangers. On August 22, 1989, he earned his 5000th strikeout. In 1990 he threw his sixth no-hitter on June 11 against the Oakland A's, then picked up his 300th career victory on July 31 against the Milwaukee Brewers. On May 1, 1991, he added a seventh no-hitter when he turned the trick on the Toronto Blue Jays. Greg Myers of the Angels was Ryan's 5,714th and final strikeout victim on September 17, 1993. Five days later, he made his final start as he tore a ligament in his elbow. His final pitch in the majors, coming after the injury, was clocked at 98 mph.

Ryan finished his career with a record of 324-292 in 807 games, 773 of which were starts. He threw 222 complete games and 61 shutouts, walking a league record 2,795 hitters to go with his 5,714 strikeouts. He was inducted into the Baseball Hall of Fame in 1999.

Pitcher Nolan Ryan #34 of the Houston Astros pitching in Shea Stadium in 1986 in Flushing, NY.

PLAYER STATISTICS:
Position: Pitcher
Born: January 31, 1947
Batted: Right
Threw: Right
Win-Loss 324-292
SO: 5714
ERA: 3.19
TEAMS:
New York Mets (1966, 1968-1971)
California Angels (1972-1979)
Houston Astros (1980-1988)
Texas Rangers (1989-1993)
HIGHLIGHTS/AWARDS:
• 8x All-Star
• No-hitters: 7 (most all time)
• 5,714 career strikeouts (most all time)
NOTEWORTHY:
Member of the National Baseball Hall of Fame
Elected 1999 (Vote 98.8%, first ballot)
Astros

BASEBALL GREATS

WARREN SPAHN

Warren Edward Spahn was a left-handed pitcher who played 21 seasons of Major League Baseball, all in the National League. Born in Buffalo, New York, on April 23, 1921, Spahn was an astonishingly consistent and durable pitcher and is credited as one of the best left-handed pitchers in Major League Baseball history. Throughout his career he secured 20 wins in 13 different seasons, tying Christy Mathewson for the most in National League history. He won a total of 363 games, more games than any other left-handed pitcher and the fifth-highest winning tally in Major League Baseball history. He gathered a 23-7 win-loss record at the age of 42.

Spahn was signed with the Boston Braves out of high school in 1940 and was invited to spring training after he won 19 games in the minor league in 1941. He debuted in the major league in 1942 but his major league career stalled when Casey Stengel demoted him after the left-hander refused to sweep back Pee Wee Reese in an exhibition game. Stengel's decision proved to be the worst mistake he ever made as Spahn went 17-12 with a 1.96 ERA at Hartford that season while the Braves finished in seventh place. In 1943 Spahn joined the United States Army to serve in World War II; his service earned him a Bronze Star, a Purple Heart and a battlefield commission.

After the war, Spahn returned to baseball in 1946. He emerged as one of baseball's best pitchers in 1947 with a 21-10 record and topped the league with a 2.33 ERA. He won 20 or more games in 13 of the next 17 seasons. Spahn helped pitch the Braves to a 1957 World Series championship and National League pennants in 1948 and 1958. While with the Braves, Spahn led the National League in victories eight times, including five seasons in a row from 1957-1961, and led the league in strikeouts from 1949-1952. In his two best seasons, Spahn was 23-7 and led the league with a 2.10 ERA in 1953 at age 32. He matched that record a decade later at 42 but he had a 2.60 ERA in 1963.

In 1965 Spahn played his final season with the New York Mets and the San Francisco Giants, winning seven games combined for the Mets and Giants. He then pitched in Mexico and the minors before finally retiring in 1967 at 46. Throughout his career he pitched two no-hitters, won 3 ERA titles and has appeared in 14 National League All-Star Games, the most of any pitcher in the twentieth century. Spahn was named *The Sporting News'* Pitcher of the Year in 1953, 1957, 1958 and in 1961; he was also named as the winner of the Cy Young Award in 1957 and the Lou Gehrig Memorial Award in 1961. The Atlanta Braves retired Spahn's jersey number 21 in 1965. Spahn was elected to the Baseball Hall of Fame in 1973, his first year of eligibility, receiving nearly 83 percent of the votes. In 1999 *The Sporting News* ranked Spahn as 21 out of 100 Greatest Baseball Players of all time. He was also elected as a member of the Major League Baseball All-Century Team with 337,215 votes. Spahn passed away at the age of 82 on November 24, 2003.

Milwaukee Braves player Warren Spahn winding up to throw a pitch.

PLAYER STATISTICS:

Position:	Starting Pitcher
Born:	April 23, 1921
Died:	November 24, 2003 (aged 82)
Batted:	Left
Threw:	Left
Win-Loss	363-245
ERA:	3.09
SO:	2583

TEAMS:

Boston/Milwaukee Braves (1942 - 1964)
New York Mets (1965)
San Francisco Giants (1965)

HIGHLIGHTS/AWARDS:

- Jersey number (#21) Retired by the Atlanta Braves
- 14x NL All-Star
- The Sporting News Pitcher of the Year (1953, 1957-1958, 1961)
- Cy Young Award (1957)
- Lou Gehrig Memorial Award (1961)
- 6th on the all-time list for career wins
- Winningest pitcher in the live-ball era
- Two career no-hitters

NOTEWORTHY:

- Member of the National Baseball Hall of Fame Elected 1973 (Vote 82.89%)

BASEBALL GREATS

TED WILLIAMS

There may be no better example of a pure hitter than the Splendid Splinter himself, Ted Williams. Williams made hitting seem easy, holding the highest career average (.344) for any player with at least 500 career home runs. It's easy to overlook that he lost three years of his prime due to World War II. While never leading the league in hits, he led in average six times and is the last man in baseball history to hit over .400, when he hit .406 in 1941 en route to capturing the Triple Crown.

The Red Sox signed Williams as an amateur free agent following the 1936 season. He made his big league debut on April 20, 1939, going 1-for-4 with a double and two strikeouts in a 2-0 Yankees victory on Opening Day. Williams finished the season hitting .327 with 31 home runs and was the first rookie to lead the league in RBIs with 145. He finished fourth in the MVP voting and would have been Rookie of the Year, had the award existed then. He made his first All-Star appearance in 1940, finishing the year with a .344 average, 23 home runs and 113 RBIs.

The 1941 season may have been the high-water mark of Williams' career. After breaking his ankle during spring training, he was limited to pinch-hitting the first two weeks of the year. He ripped off a 22-game hitting streak in May and June, with his average reaching .430 at one point. Heading into the final day of the season, where the Red Sox had a doubleheader with the Philadelphia A's, Williams was hitting .39955, which would round up to .400 if he didn't play. Williams chose to play, going 6-for-8 to finish at .406, the first .400 season in the majors since Bill Terry hit .401 in 1930. Williams also led the league in home runs with 37, while finishing fourth in RBIs with 120. He finished second to Joe DiMaggio in the MVP voting that year. Williams claimed the AL Triple Crown in 1942, leading the league with a .356 average along with 36 home runs and 137 RBIs. He would miss the next three seasons serving the United States Marine Corps in World War II.

Williams returned with a vengeance in 1946, claiming his first MVP Award while hitting .342 with 38 home runs and 123 RBIs. He made his only appearance in the World Series that year and went 5-for-25, struggling after being hit in the elbow by a pitch in an exhibition game in early October. Boston succumbed in seven games, and the defeat was painful for Williams. The 1947 season saw him claim the Triple Crown again, hitting .343 with 32 home runs and 114 RBIs, but was again denied the MVP, losing to DiMaggio by one vote.

Williams would lead the league in hitting in 1948, 1957 and 1958. He missed the Triple Crown in 1949 after losing the batting title by .0002 to George Kell. Williams hit .343 with 43 home runs and 159 RBIs. Boston lost a one-game lead at the end of the season to the Yankees and would not finish higher than third place the rest of Williams' career. He suffered a broken arm in the 1950 All-Star Game that would cost him most of the second half of the season.

Williams missed the better part of two more seasons in 1952 and 1953 as he was recalled by the Marine Corps as an inactive reserve during the Korean War. He played just six games in 1952 and 37 in 1953. He broke his collarbone in spring training in 1954, missing the first six weeks of the season. Williams played until 1960, winning batting titles at the ages of 39 and 40. His final at-bat came on September 28, 1960, against the Washington Senators. He blasted a home run, his 29th of the season, to deep center field off Jack Fisher to bring the Red Sox within 4-3. They would score twice more in the bottom of the ninth to claim a 5-4 victory in Williams' final contest. He did not play in the final three Red Sox games on the road at Yankee Stadium.

Williams finished his career with a .344 average, 521 home runs and 1839 RBIs. He led the league in hitting six times, and in on-base percentage 12 times. He died of cardiac arrest on July 5, 2002, at the age of 83.

Hall of Fame slugger Ted Williams #9 of the Boston Red Soxs hits one of his 521 career home runs during a game against the Cleveland Indians at Cleveland Municipal Stadium in Cleveland, OH.

PLAYER STATISTICS:
Position: Outfielder
Born: August 30, 1918
Died: July 5, 2002 (aged 83)
Batted: Left
Threw: Right
AVG: .344
HR: 521
RBI: 1839
OBP: .482
TEAMS
Boston Red Sox (1939-1942), (1946-1952), (1953-1960)
Washington Senators (1969-1971)
Texas Rangers (1972)
HIGHLIGHTS/AWARDS:
• 2x MVP Award (1946, 1949)
• 17x All-Star - AL
• Major League Player of the Year (1941, 1942, 1947, 1949, 1957)
• AL Triple Crown (1942, 1947)
NOTEWORTHY:
• Member of the National Baseball Hall of Fame
Elected 1966 (Vote 93.38%, first ballot)
player to hit at least .400 in a season
champ in Major League

BASEBALL GREATS
CY YOUNG

There may well be no pitcher that is more well-known than Cy Young. The Cy Young Award, given every season to the best pitcher in each league, is a tribute to the statistical prowess he put together over his career, which spanned the late nineteenth and early twentieth centuries. Bridging the gap between early and modern era baseball, he has 94 more wins than any other pitcher in major league history and holds a myriad of baseball's records for pitchers a century after playing his final game.

Young made his major league debut with the Cleveland Spiders on August 6, 1890. The Spiders had moved up from the American Association to the National League in 1889 and were trying to cultivate top-level talent. Young's first outing with the team was a three-hit shutout. On the final day of the 1890 season, he started and won both ends of a doubleheader. He would finish his rookie season with a record of 9-7 with a 3.47 ERA in 17 games, 16 of which were starts.

Young pitched for the Spiders through the 1898 season, never winning fewer than 21 games in a season. Along the way, he posted three 30-plus win campaigns, including a league-leading 36 in 1892, when he also led with a 1.93 ERA. He posted a record of 241-135 with a 3.10 ERA while with Cleveland and pitched in 420 games, 369 of which were starts. Of those 369 starts, Young threw complete games in 346 of them, 24 of which were shutouts. In 1895 the Spiders won the Temple Cup, which was a precursor to the modern World Series, over the Baltimore Orioles.

Before the 1899 season, Spiders owner Frank Robison also purchased the St. Louis Browns. Robison changed the club's name from the Browns to the Perfectos and began shifting his premium Spiders talent to St. Louis, but the Perfectos were a disappointment. Young was 45-35 in two seasons with the Perfectos, tossing 72 complete games in 77 starts. Meanwhile, the Spiders folded at the end of the 1899 season.

The AL made the transition from minor to major league status in 1901 and promptly began raiding NL rosters. Young made the jump and signed a contract worth $3,500 a year with the Boston Americans. He would win the pitching version of the Triple Crown in his first year in the AL, leading in wins (33), ERA (1.62) and strikeouts (158). He would lead the league in victories again in 1902 and 1903, winning 32 and 28 games in those seasons, respectively.

In 1903 Young and the then-Boston Pilgrims faced the Pittsburgh Pirates in the first World Series in baseball history. The series was a best-of-nine affair, and the Americans captured the first championship five games to three. The next season, Young threw the first perfect game in AL history on May 5, 1904, holding the Philadelphia Athletics without a baserunner. That was part of Young's major league-record 25.1 consecutive hitless innings pitched, a record that still stands today.

Young tossed his third no-hitter at the age of 41 in 1908, making him the oldest pitcher to do so at the time. That record would hold for 82 years, until Nolan Ryan accomplished the feat at the age of 43 in 1990. Young was traded back to Cleveland prior to the 1909 season, this time to the Naps, where he would pitch two-and-a-half seasons before closing his career with 11 starts for the Boston Rustlers. His final victory in the majors came on September 22, 1911, when he and the Rustlers shut out the Pittsburgh Pirates, 1-0.

Young finished his career with a major league-record 511 victories as well as a record 316 defeats. Young's career ERA was 2.63 in 906 games, including a record 815 starts. Of those starts, Young tossed 749 complete games and 76 shutouts. He threw three no-hitters, a perfect game, and was part of the first World Series-winning team in baseball history. Additionally, he is partially responsible for the relocation of the pitcher's mound back five feet due to how hard he could throw. He was inducted into the Baseball Hall of Fame in 1937 and died on November 4, 1955, at the age of 88.

Cy Young, pitcher for the Boston Red Sox, warms up before a game at Huntingdon Ave. Grounds in Boston.

PLAYER STATISTICS:

Position: Pitcher
Born: March 29, 1867
Died: November 4, 1955 (aged 88)
Batted: Right
Threw: Right
Win-Loss 511-316
E.R.A. 2.63
SO: 2803

TEAMS:

Cleveland Spiders (1890-1898)
St. Louis Perfectos (1899-1900)
Boston Americans/Red Sox (1901-1908)
Cleveland Naps (1909-1911)
Boston Rustlers (1911)

HIGHLIGHTS/AWARDS:

- AL Triple Crown for Pitchers (1901)
- 1st All-Time wins (511)
- 1st All-Time IP (7354 2/3)
- 1st All-Time Games Started (815)
- 1st All-Time Complete Games (749)
- Boston Red Sox Career Leader in WHIP (.97), Walks/9IP (.99) and Complete Games (275)

NOTEWORTHY:

- Member of the National Baseball Hall of Fame Elected 1937 (Vote 76.12%)

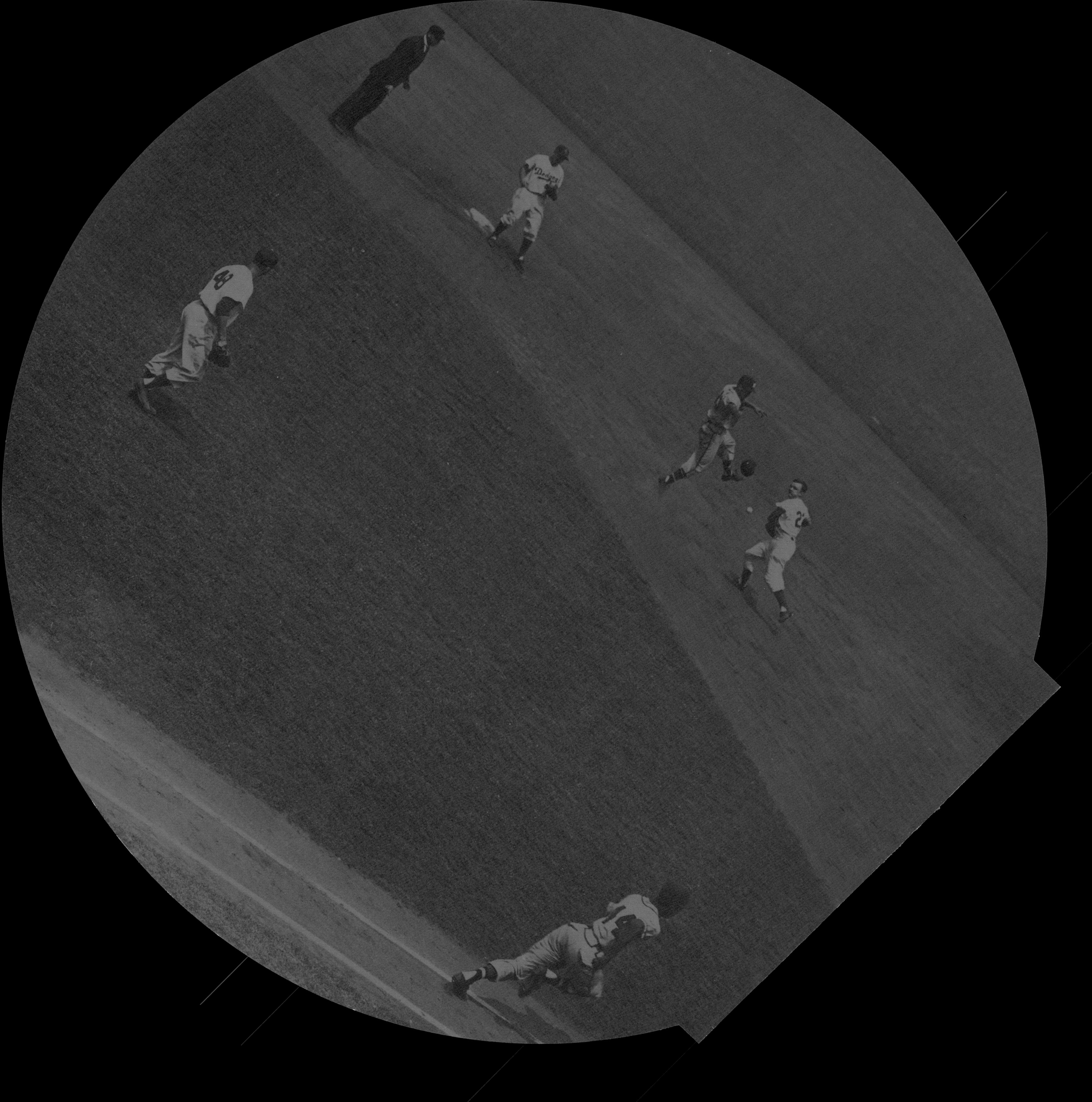

MAJOR LEAGUE TEAMS

ARIZONA DIAMONDBACKS

The Arizona Diamondbacks were an expansion team that joined the National League in 1998. They play in the NL West Division, with their home games played at Chase Field. The name of the franchise was selected prior to the ownership group even being approved for a major league team and on March 9, 1995, the franchise was awarded to Jerry Colangelo and his group at a price of $130 million.

Arizona was originally voted in to play in the AL along with expansion team Tampa Bay, but several AL teams stated they would vote to block that assignment because they would have more games out of their respective time zones. On January 16, 1997, the decision was made to add the Diamondbacks to the National League and Tampa Bay to the American League.

Arizona hired Buck Showalter, who won the AL Manager of the Year Award in 1994, as their first manager a full two years before their first game.

Arizona played the first regular season game in franchise history on March 31, 1998, against the Colorado Rockies before a crowd of 47,484 at Bank One Ballpark; the Rockies were victorious, 9-2. Travis Lee's solo home run in the sixth inning accounted for the first home run and run scored for the Diamondbacks. Arizona struggled as expected for an expansion team, finishing the year with a mark of 65-97.

In 1999 the Diamondbacks signed flame-throwing left-handed pitcher Randy Johnson. He went 103-49 in his first stint with the team from 1999 through 2004. Arizona had a 100-win campaign in their second year, winning the NL West Division for the first time. They fell short in the playoffs, however, losing to the Mets three games to one in the NLDS. After a disappointing 2000 season, Showalter was replaced by Bob Brenly.

The 2001 season saw Arizona return to prominence behind the 1-2 punch of Johnson and Curt Schilling. The team won 92 games and their second NL West title. They edged the St. Louis Cardinals, three games to two, in the NLDS and then handled the Atlanta Braves in five games in the NLCS. That put Arizona in their first World Series in their fourth year. They rallied with two runs in the ninth inning of Game Seven off Yankees closer Mariano Rivera to win, 3-2, for their only World Series championship as of 2014.

The Diamondbacks won the NL West again in 2002 after posting 98 victories, but were wiped out in three straight games by the Cardinals in the NLDS. Johnson claimed his fourth consecutive Cy Young Award that year. Arizona fell to 84-78 and third place in 2003, and Schilling was dealt to Boston after the season. The team hit rock bottom in 2004, winning just 51 games. After the season Johnson was dealt to the Yankees as the team again began to rebuild.

Arizona has made the playoffs just twice since 2002, losing in the NLCS in 2007 and in the NLDS in 2011. In 2011 they had 94 victories, a 29-game improvement over 2010, and in both 2012 and 2013 the team finished 81-81. They were second place in the NL West in 2013 but failed to make the postseason. Ace pitcher Patrick Corbin suffered a torn ulnar collateral ligament in his elbow and missed the 2014 season.

The Diamondbacks opened up the 2014 season dropping their first two games against the Los Angeles Dodgers in Sydney, Australia. It was the start of a long, dreadful season for the team, as they finished the year 64-98 and in the basement of the NL West. Fan favorites Gerardo Parra and Martin Prado were dealt to Milwaukee and the Yankees; starting pitcher Brandon McCarthy was sent to New York as well.

In the offseason, the Diamondbacks have been active in an effort to rebuild their pitching staff. They acquired Rubby De La Rosa and Allen Webster, who pitched as a starter and a reliever in 2014 for Boston. Their versatility could help an Arizona pitching staff that was 27th in the majors with 75 quality starts last season. To add some pop in the lineup, they signed Cuban outfielder Yasmany Tomas to a six year, $68.5 million deal.

Paul Goldschmidt #44 of the Arizona Diamondbacks bats during the game against the Philadelphia Phillies on July 27, 2014, at Citizens Bank Park in Philadelphia, PA. The Phillies defeated the Diamondbacks 4-2.

FIRST YEAR OF EXISTENCE: 1998
OWNER: KEN KENDRICK, JEFFREY ROYER
MANAGER: CHIP HALE (OCTOBER 13, 2014-PRESENT)

MAJOR LEAGUE TEAMS

ATLANTA BRAVES

The Atlanta Braves are one of the oldest franchises in Major League Baseball, having been in existence since the 1876 season. They have had many different monikers but have been known as the Braves, albeit it in different cities, since 1912. Through 2014, they have won three World Series championships and 17 NL pennants. Atlanta is frequently called "America's Team" due to their coverage on cable channel TBS during the 1980s and 1990s.

The oldest continuously playing team in major league history, the Braves played in the first game in NL history when as the Boston Redcaps, they defeated the Philadelphia Athletics 6-5 on April 22, 1876. The franchise claimed eight NL pennants during the nineteenth century and was a NL powerhouse during that time. The team played as the Boston Red Stockings through 1881 before changing their name to the Beaneaters. They then had a four-year stint as the Doves from 1907 to 1910, and one year as the Rustlers in 1911 before adopting the name Braves. The team appeared in just two World Series while playing in Boston, winning in four games over the Philadelphia Athletics in 1914 and, 34 years later, losing the 1948 Series to the Cleveland Indians, four games to two. The Braves had Babe Ruth for the final two months of his career in hopes that he would help boost attendance in 1935, but he was well beyond his prime. He retired on June 1, and the Braves finished with a record of 38-115. Following the debacle of 1935, the team changed its name to the Bees, which it remained through 1940.

As attendance declined, owner Lou Perini announced on March 13, 1953, that the team would be moving to Milwaukee. The Braves were a hit there, drawing a then-league record 1.8 million fans and winning 92 games behind young stars Eddie Mathews and Hank Aaron. The team claimed their first pennant in 1957, and behind Lew Burdette's three complete game victories, won their second World Series crown in seven games over the Yankees. Milwaukee won the pennant again in 1958, but the Yankees took the World Series.

Times would be more difficult for the rest of the team's stay in Milwaukee. Perini sold the team in 1962, and in 1963 they finished sixth in the 10-team NL, their only "second division" finish while in Milwaukee. The Braves announced their intention to move to Atlanta in 1965 but a court injunction forced them to play that season in Milwaukee, and they would not make the move until 1966.

The Braves won the first NL West Division title after expansion led to divisional play in 1969 but were knocked out by the Mets in the NLCS. Atlanta struggled over the next decade, posting just two winning seasons between 1970 and 1981. A high point during these low times came on April 8, 1974, when Hank Aaron hit career home run number 715, breaking Ruth's all-time record.

After winning the NL West in 1969, the Braves did not return to the playoffs until 1982, where they were again swept in the NLCS. They posted seven straight losing seasons between 1984 and 1990 before Bobby Cox returned for his second stint as manager of the club. Under his leadership, Atlanta claimed 14 straight division titles (the 1994 season was wiped out by the strike). Despite all that success, they won just one World Series in 1995 over the Cleveland Indians.

Atlanta went 96-66 in the 2013 regular season and earned their 18th division championship with a 5-2 triumph over the Cubs on September 22. The Braves made the playoffs for the third time in four seasons but lost the NLDS, three games to one, to the Dodgers.

The 2014 campaign was a disappointment for the Braves as they finished 79-83 for their first losing record since 2008. They were done in by poor offensive production, finishing second-worst in the major leagues with just 573 runs. In the offseason Atlanta signed outfielder Nick Markakis to a four-year, $45 million deal, as well as relief pitcher Jim Johnson and utility infielder Alberto Callaspo to one-year deals.

Craig Kimbrel #46 of the Atlanta Braves pitches in the ninth inning against the Philadelphia Phillies at Turner Field on September 3, 2014, in Atlanta, GA.

KIMBREL
46
FIRST YEAR OF EXISTENCE: 1876
OWNER: LIBERTY MEDIA
MANAGER: FREDI GONZALEZ (OCTOBER 13, 2010-PRESENT)

MAJOR LEAGUE TEAMS

BALTIMORE ORIOLES

The Baltimore Orioles have been a part of Major League Baseball since 1901, though they have only been the Orioles since 1954. One of the original eight charter members of the AL, Baltimore has claimed three World Series championships and seven pennants in its history. The Orioles have been a bit of a perennial also-ran for a good chunk of their existence, not making their first playoff appearance until 1944.

The team began as the Milwaukee Brewers in 1901, and spent just one season in the city. They went 48-89 and then were finished in Wisconsin. They moved to St. Louis in time for the 1902 season and became known as the St. Louis Browns.

They finished second in the AL in that year, going 78-58, but quickly fell apart. They would finish no higher than fourth in the AL again until the 1921 season, when they were third. The team lost at least 90 games seven times in that span, including three straight seasons with at least 101 losses between 1910 and 1912.

The Browns made their first World Series appearance in 1944 after winning 89 games during the regular season, but they lost in six games to their rival, the St. Louis Cardinals. They finished 81-70 in 1945 and didn't post another winning season in St. Louis through 1953. The club moved to Baltimore in 1954 despite a crowd of 350,000 lining a parade route that led to Memorial Stadium. The team would not post a winning record in Baltimore until 1960.

The Orioles finally put things together in 1966, a year after acquiring Frank Robinson. They won their first AL pennant in Baltimore that year and swept the Los Angeles Dodgers to claim their first World Series crown. The 1966 season began a terrific era of baseball in Baltimore. From 1969 through 1974, they made the playoffs five times. They won 109 games in 1969, the first regular season with divisional play after expansion. After beating the Twins in the ALCS, Baltimore was stunned by the Mets in five games in the World Series. The Orioles came back in 1970 to win 108 regular season games and then defeated the Cincinnati Reds for their second World Series crown in five years.

Baltimore had four 20-game winners on their pitching staff in 1971 and made their third straight World Series appearance. Again, they were rebuffed, losing to the Pittsburgh Pirates in seven games. Baltimore won division titles in 1973 and 1974 but lost to the Oakland A's both times in the ALCS.

Baltimore claimed the AL pennant in 1979 but were turned away by the Pirates in seven games. They posted a winning season every year from 1968 to 1985, winning at least 97 games eight times in that span. The Orioles claimed the 1983 World Series, dispatching the Philadelphia Phillies in five games. The team lost their first 21 games in 1988 and sunk to a record of 54-107.

The Orioles returned to the playoffs in 1996, when they claimed the AL wild card. They reached the ALCS in both 1996 and 1997 but were upended by the Yankees and Indians respectively.

The Orioles snapped a 14-season playoff drought in 2012 but were knocked off 3-2 by the Yankees in the ALDS. Baltimore put together a second consecutive winning season in 2013 as they went 85-77 but finished third in the AL East and missed the playoffs. The Orioles posted back-to-back winning seasons for the first time since 1996 and 1997, and first baseman Chris Davis slammed a club record 53 home runs on the season.

Baltimore had a terrific season in 2014 as they won their first AL East title since 1997. They finished the year 96-66, 12 games ahead of the second-place Yankees, despite the loss of key players like Manny Machado and Matt Wieters.

The Orioles swept the Detroit Tigers in the ALDS but ran out of magic in the ALCS, as they were swept by the Kansas City Royals. It's been a quiet offseason for Baltimore, who hasn't made any major moves to improve the club but has taken some significant hits, losing slugging outfielder Nelson Cruz, reliever Andrew Miller and outfielder Nick Markakis.

Adam Jones #10 of the Baltimore Orioles takes the field against the Minnesota Twins at Oriole Park at Camden Yards on September 1, 2014, in Baltimore, MD. The Minnesota Twins won, 6-4.

FIRST YEAR OF EXISTENCE: 1901
OWNER: PETER ANGELOS
MANAGER: BUCK SHOWALTER (JULY 29, 2010-PRESENT)

MAJOR LEAGUE TEAMS

BOSTON RED SOX

The Boston Red Sox have been a part of Major League Baseball since 1901 and were a charter member of the AL. First named the Boston Americans, the team became the Red Sox after the 1907 season. The franchise has eight World Series championships and 13 AL pennants.

The Red Sox posted winning marks in each of their first five seasons in the AL through 1905. They claimed the 1903 AL pennant, the first in franchise history, and played in the first World Series in major league history against the Pittsburgh Pirates, winning five games to three. Cy Young, baseball's winningest pitcher and a member of the club, threw the first pitch in World Series play.

Boston won four World Series titles between 1912 and 1918. They defeated the New York Giants in 1912, the Philadelphia Phillies in 1915, repeated as champions against the Brooklyn Robins in 1916, and then defeated the Chicago Cubs in 1918. On December 26, 1919, the Red Sox made a franchise-damaging mistake when Harry Frazee sold Babe Ruth to the Yankees. The Yankees became an instant powerhouse behind Ruth and Boston did not win another World Series title for 86 years.

In the Ted Williams era, the Red Sox were marginally better but made just one World Series appearance in his career in 1946, losing in seven games to the St. Louis Cardinals. The Red Sox won at least 94 games in three straight seasons from 1948 to 1950, but were unable to win the AL pennant.

Following eight losing seasons in a row through 1966, Boston captured the AL flag in 1967 behind Carl Yastrzemski's Triple Crown but fell in seven games to the Cardinals. That was the first of 16 consecutive winning seasons for the Red Sox through 1982. Although they won more than 90 games five times in the run, they only made the playoffs twice. They captured the pennant in 1975 but lost the World Series in seven games to the Cincinnati Reds. Boston forced a one-game playoff with the Yankees in 1978 but lost 5-4.

Boston won 108 games in 1986 and rallied from a three-games-to-one deficit in the ALCS to stun the California Angels and advance to the World Series for the first time in 11 years. Again, the "curse" of Babe Ruth came back to bite Boston, and the Mets claimed the Series in seven games.

Boston won the AL East in 1988 and 1990 but was swept in the ALCS both years by the Oakland A's. They returned to the playoffs in 1995 but lost in the divisional round to the Cleveland Indians; Cleveland eliminated Boston again in the 1998 ALDS. In 1999 Boston made it to the ALCS but was shelved by the Yankees in five games.

Boston made the playoffs six times from 2003 to 2009. They lost the 2003 ALCS in seven games to the Yankees but came back in the 2004 ALCS, defeating the Yankees in seven games to punch their ticket to the World Series. They swept the Cardinals in four straight games to clinch their first Series title in 86 years.

The Red Sox won their second World Series in four years in 2007 when they beat the Colorado Rockies in four games. Boston lost the 2008 ALCS to Tampa Bay and the 2009 ALDS to the Angels. The team finished third in 2010 and 2011 to miss the playoffs, and they bottomed out in 2012, finishing 69-93. In 2013 Boston won 97 games in the regular season and went on to their third World Series title in 10 years, beating the Cardinals in six games.

The 2014 campaign was a nightmare for Boston. They finished 71-91 and 25 games behind the division-winning Orioles. Boston dealt longtime ace Jon Lester and Jonny Gomes to Oakland at the trade deadline in exchange for Yoenis Cespedes in a move that didn't really work out as well as either side would have hoped. Boston did sign Cuban outfielder Rusney Castillo as they began looking to the future.

Boston has been proactive in the offseason in an effort to get back to the postseason. They acquired Pablo Sandoval, Hanley Ramirez, left-handed starter Wade Miley and Rick Porcello, as well as Justin Masterson and catcher Ryan Hanigan.

Outfielder Carl (Yaz) Yaztrzemski #8 of the Boston Red Sox bats during a 1967 World Series game in Fenway Park in October 1967 against the St. Louis Cardinals in Boston, MA.

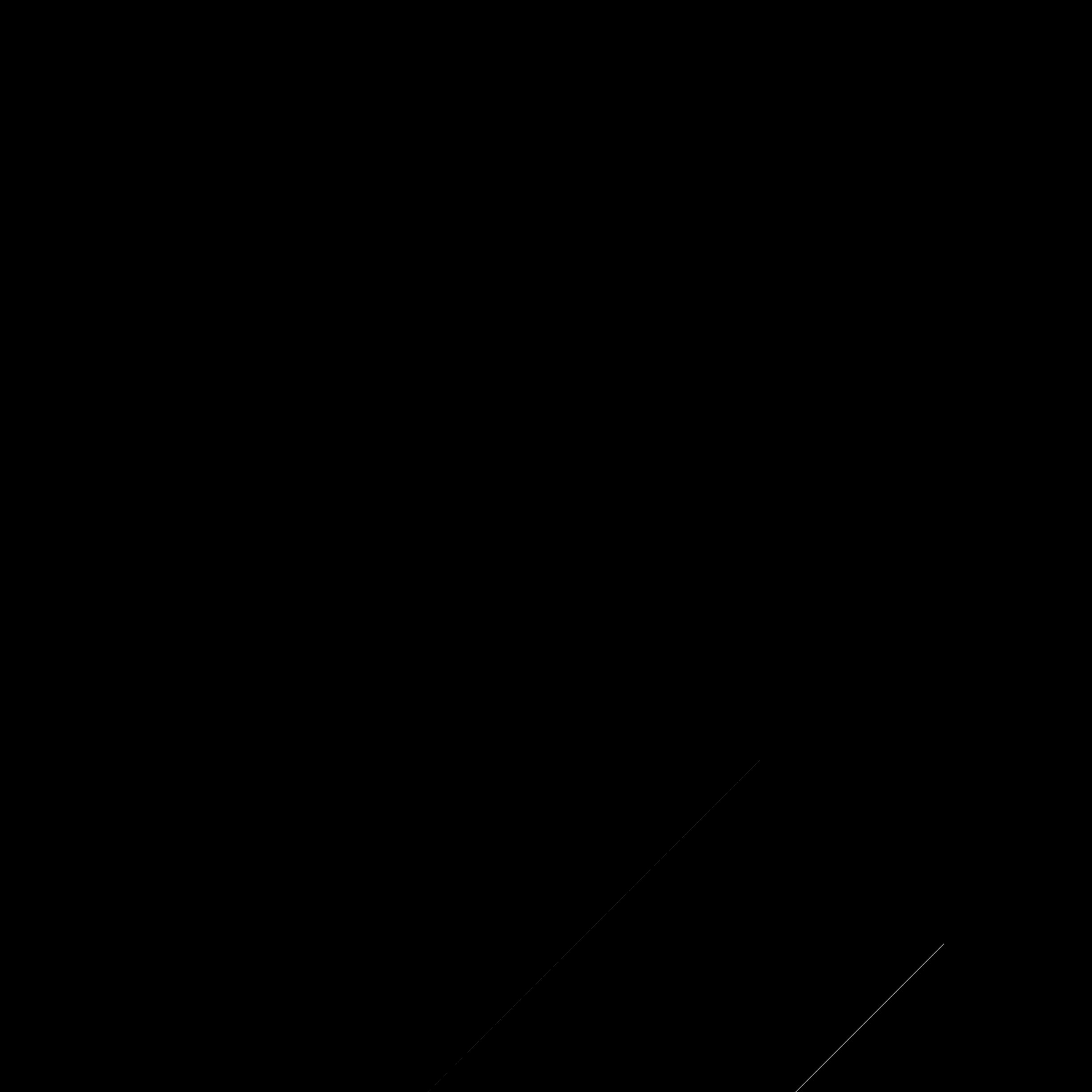

MAJOR LEAGUE TEAMS

CHICAGO CUBS

The Chicago Cubs have been a part of Major League Baseball since the start of the NL in 1876. The team has had some high points, but the dynasty years at the beginning of the twentieth century seem like a distant memory. They have not won a World Series since 1908 and have failed to even appear in one since a 1945 loss to the Detroit Tigers.

The Cubs were originally known as the Chicago White Stockings and became the Colts in 1889. The franchise claimed six pennants between 1876 and 1886 and had seven more winning seasons through 1897, but they could not claim another pennant. The franchise was known as the Orphans from 1898 to 1902 before adopting the Cubs moniker.

The Cubs were a powerhouse team between 1904 and 1913, winning 88 games or more in each of those seasons, including four seasons with at least 104 wins. In 1906 the Cubs had a major league-record 116 victories in the season and made their first trip to the World Series, where they lost in six games to their rivals, the White Sox. In 1907 the Cubs claimed their first World Series championship with a sweep of the Detroit Tigers and followed that up with a repeat in 1908, this time dispatching the Tigers in five games.

Chicago returned to the World Series in 1910 for the fourth time in five years. This time, there would be no October magic, as the Philadelphia Athletics handled the Cubs in five games.

The Cubs lost the 1918 Series in six games to the Red Sox and fared no better in 1929, 1932 or 1935, losing to Philadelphia, the Yankees and the Tigers, respectively. The Cubs returned to the World Series in 1938 but were again denied by the Yankees.

The 1945 World Series was another chance at redemption for the Cubs, but they lost in seven games to Detroit. They haven't returned to the Fall Classic since. In the first year of divisional play in 1969, the Cubs led the newly created NL East by 8.5 games over St. Louis and 9.5 games over the New York Mets on August 19. The team fell apart down the stretch, however. Some fans believe that a black cat let loose at Shea Stadium on September 9 is to blame.

The 1984 season was another unfortunate event for Chicago. The Cubs won the first two games of the NLCS against the San Diego Padres and needed just one win in their final three games to go to the World Series. Thirty years later, they're still looking. The Cubs lost the NLCS in five games in 1989 to the San Francisco Giants. They returned to the playoffs in 1998, winning a one-game playoff to claim the wild card, but were swept away by the Braves in the NLDS. The 2003 season was more heartbreak for Chicago: after beating the Braves in five games in the NLDS, the club faced the Florida Marlins in the NLCS and led three games to two with a 3-0 lead in the eighth inning of Game Six before the wheels fell off. The Marlins evened the series and won Game Seven to advance to the World Series. The Cubs went into a tailspin after that, making the playoffs in 2007 and 2008 but losing both times in the NLDS.

Chicago struggled to their fourth straight losing season as they went 66-96 in 2013. While that marked a five-game improvement over the 2012 season, two major building blocks in the lineup, Starlin Castro and Anthony Rizzo, struggled during the season. The 2014 season went about as well as could be expected for a young Chicago team. While they finished in the basement of the NL Central for the third straight year, they did improve to 73-89. Chicago acquired top prospects Addison Russell and Billy McKinney along with Dan Straily. Anthony Rizzo had a bounce-back season as he hit .286 with 32 homers and Starlin Castro was playing well before going down with an injury that cost him the final month of the season. In the offseason, the Cubs made a big splash in free agency by signing ace starter Jon Lester, catcher Miguel Montero and second baseman Tommy La Stella. The four-year, $500 million renovation of Wrigley Field began at the conclusion of the 2014 season as well.

Pitcher Ferguson Jenkins #31of the Chicago Cubs signs autographs for the fans before the start of an Major League Baseball game circa 1973 at Wrigley Field in Chicago, IL. Jenkins played for the Cubs from 1966-73, 1982-83.

FIRST YEAR OF EXISTENCE: 1876
OWNER: THOMAS S. RICKETTS
MANAGER: JOE MADDON (NOVEMBER 3, 2014-PRESENT)

MAJOR LEAGUE TEAMS

CHICAGO WHITE SOX

One of the eight charter members of the American League, the Chicago White Sox have been a part of Major League Baseball since 1901. Like their crosstown rivals the Chicago Cubs, the White Sox have had their share of struggles. The team has claimed three World Series championships and six AL pennants in franchise history.

The franchise began as the Sioux City Cornhuskers in the Western League in 1894. When the Western League became the AL in time for the 1900 season it was still a minor league, but the NL approved a team to be placed in Chicago. The team stayed with the AL when it declared itself a major league in 1901 and claimed the first pennant in AL history that year, finishing with a record of 83-53-1.

The White Sox made their first World Series appearance in 1906 against the Cubs and won their first title four games to two. They returned to the World Series in 1917 after winning a franchise-record 100 games in the regular season. The team dispatched the New York Giants in six games to claim their second championship. They would not claim another until 2005.

In 1919 the White Sox returned to the Fall Classic and were heavily favored against the Cincinnati Reds. Major amounts of money were bet on the Reds, leading to whispers of the World Series being fixed. The whispers grew louder as the Series wore on, and the Reds prevailed, five games to three. An investigation was carried out the following year and, in what was known as the "Black Sox Scandal," eight players were banned for life from the sport: Shoeless Joe Jackson, Eddie Cicotte, Chick Gandil, Happy Felsch, Lefty Williams, Swede Risberg, Buck Weaver and Fred McMullin. Jackson's involvement has been disputed for decades, but his ban has not been overturned.

Starting in 1921, Chicago didn't finish higher than fourth until 1937 and would not win another pennant until 1959. They celebrated their first trip to the playoffs since 1919 with an 11-0 shellacking of the Los Angeles Dodgers in Game One of the World Series, but proceeded to drop the Series in six games. The team would win 94, 98 and 95 games in 1964, 1965 and 1966 respectively but would not return to the playoffs again until 1983.

The White Sox were upended in the 1983 ALCS by the Baltimore Orioles in four games, and in their next appearance in 1993, it was the Toronto Blue Jays that did the honors of knocking Chicago out of the playoff picture. The team made the playoffs once in the Jerry Manuel era, but lost in three straight games of the 2000 ALDS to the Seattle Mariners.

The White Sox had extended success under fiery manager and former player Ozzie Guillen, who led them to their first World Series victory in 88 years when the club beat the Houston Astros in 2005. They were unable to keep the momentum, though, and made the playoffs just once in the following six seasons. That appearance came in 2008, when Chicago lost in four games in the ALDS to Tampa Bay.

Chicago missed the postseason for the fifth straight season as they went 63-99 and finished last in the AL Central in 2013. Their offense took a precipitous drop as they scored 150 fewer runs while allowing 47 more than they did in 2012. It was their first season of at least 95 losses since 1976. The 2014 season was another losing campaign for the White Sox but they did improve 10 games in the standings to go 73-89. Jose Abreu won the AL Rookie of the Year honors after hitting .317 with 36 homers and 107 RBIs in 145 games; he also made the All-Star Game.

In an effort to try to set things in motion for a successful 2015 campaign, the White Sox were extremely proactive once free agency opened up. They signed reliever Zach Duke, slugging first baseman Adam LaRoche, closer David Robertson and outfielder Melky Cabrera. In a major deal to add a frontline starter to their rotation, the White Sox sent Marcus Semien, Rangel Ravelo, Josh Phegley and Chris Bassitt to the A's in exchange for Jeff Samardzija and Michael Ynoa.

Jose Abreu #79 of the Chicago White Sox bats against the Tampa Bay Rays on April 27, 2014, at U.S. Cellular Field in Chicago, IL. The White Sox defeated the Rays 9-2.

FIRST YEAR OF EXISTENCE: 1901
OWNERS: JERRY REINSDORF AND EDDIE EINHORN
MANAGER: ROBIN VENTURA (OCTOBER 6, 2011-PRESENT)

MAJOR LEAGUE TEAMS

CINCINNATI REDS

The Cincinnati Reds have been a part of Major League Baseball since the 1890 season when they joined the National League. The Reds have claimed five World Series championships and nine NL pennants in their history. Other than a brief stint as the Cincinnati Redlegs between 1953 and 1958, they have held fast to the Reds nickname since joining the NL.

The Reds played eight seasons in the American Association, of which they were a founding member, as the Red Stockings. They won the first pennant in league history and finished second in both 1885 and 1887 before jumping to the NL for the 1890 season. Despite a 77-55 record in their first season, the Reds finished just fourth in the league. They would finish no better than third in their first quarter century in the NL.

In 1919 the club seemed to break out of their doldrums, winning the NL pennant after going 96-54 in the regular season. They were a heavy underdog in the World Series against the White Sox and there were large amounts of money being wagered on the Reds, leading some to think that the fix was in. The Reds claimed their first World Series with a five-games-to-three victory. The 1920 investigation, which led to eight White Sox players being banned from baseball for life, tarnished the championship victory.

The Reds finished second in the NL in 1922, 1923 and 1926, but by 1931 they were a fixture near the bottom of the league. They returned to the Fall Classic in 1939 but were battered in four straight games by the Yankees.

Cincinnati made the World Series again in 1940 and claimed their second Series championship with a seven-game defeat of the Detroit Tigers. Afterwards, the Reds slipped into also-ran status. Barring a second-place finish in 1943, they were never better than third and finished in the second division of the NL 13 times over the next two decades.

The Reds finally claimed another pennant in 1961 but again were run over by the Yankees in the World Series. The team returned to the World Series in both 1970 and 1972, but they were knocked out by the Baltimore Orioles and the Oakland A's, respectively. A stunning five-game loss in the 1973 NLCS to the Mets did little to improve the fans' morale.

The Big Red Machine was in full swing by the mid-1970s, and the team claimed back-to-back World Series crowns in 1975 and 1976. Cincinnati bested the Red Sox in a thrilling seven-game series in 1975 before sweeping the Yankees in four straight games the next year. The Reds had winning records throughout the remainder of the decade, but after 1976 their lone playoff appearance was the 1979 NLCS, which they lost to the Pittsburgh Pirates. It would be 11 years before they would return to the playoffs.

In 1990 Cincinnati claimed the NL West crown. The Reds won the pennant and then surprisingly swept away Oakland to claim their most recent World Series championship. The team has returned to the playoffs just four times since, losing the 1995 NLCS to Atlanta, the 2010 NLDS to Philadelphia, the 2012 NLDS to San Francisco, and the 2013 NL Wild Card game to Pittsburgh.

Cincinnati regressed seven games from their division-winning 2012 season but still went 90-72 in 2013. That record was only good for third place in the NL Central thanks to the sudden emergence of the Pirates. Jay Bruce led the team by drilling 32 homers and driving in 109 runs while Brandon Phillips had 18 homers and 103 RBIs on the season.

Injuries and decline by some of their stars hurt the Reds as they finished the 2014 season with a 76-86 record and in fourth place in the NL Central. The offseason has been one of change for Cincinnati as they've been cutting payroll in an effort to start a quasi-rebuild. Mat Latos was dealt to Miami for Chad Wallach and Anthony DeSclafani while Alfredo Simon went to Detroit in a deal that sent Eugenio Suarez and Jonathon Crawford to the Reds. On December 31, the Reds sent Ben Lively to Philadelphia in exchange for outfielder Marlon Byrd and cash.

Johnny Cueto #47 of the Cincinnati Reds pitches in the eighth inning of the game against the St. Louis Cardinals at Great American Ball Park on September 11, 2014, in Cincinnati, OH. The Reds won the game 1-0.

FIRST YEAR OF EXISTENCE: 1882
OWNER: BOB CASTELLINI
MANAGER: BRYAN PRICE (OCTOBER 22, 2013-PRESENT)

CLEVELAND INDIANS

The Cleveland Indians have been on the scene in Major League Baseball since 1901 and were one of the eight charter members of the American League. Cleveland began as the Grand Rapids Rustlers of the Western League in 1894. The Western League became the American League in 1900 and remained a minor league organization for that season. The team moved to Cleveland that year and was renamed the Lake Shores. When the AL became a major league in 1901, the team was known as the Bluebirds.

The team would become the Bronchos in 1902 and then the Naps in 1903. After the 1914 season they settled on the Indians.

Cleveland hasn't seen a plethora of success; the franchise has just two World Series championships and five AL pennants to its credit.

The Indians had three second-place finishes between 1901 and 1919, but it was not until the 1920 season that the team earned their first AL pennant. They took the World Series that year, defeating the Brooklyn Robins five games to two. They won their second and, to date, last World Series championship 28 years later in 1948 with a six-game victory over the Boston Braves.

Cleveland returned to the World Series in 1954 but was swept by the Giants. One of the most famous plays in baseball history took place in Game One of that Series. With the score tied at 2 in the eighth inning at the Polo Grounds, Cleveland had two runners on and no one out with Vic Wertz at the plate. Wertz hammered a 2-1 pitch from reliever Don Liddle to deep center field.

In most ballparks, Wertz's 240-plus foot blast would have been a three-run home run, but the Polo Grounds had ridiculous dimensions in the power alleys (450 feet in left center field, 449 in right center) and to dead center field (483 feet to the fence). Center fielder Willie Mays ran after the drive and caught it, preventing any runs from scoring on the play. The Giants won the game, 5-2, and the Indians never were really in the Series the rest of the way.

The team managed three second-place finishes during the rest of the decade, but did not claim another pennant. Once the 1950s gave way to the 1960s, Cleveland was a moribund franchise with little to cheer about. From 1960 to 1993, the Indians finished no higher than third, pulling that off just once in 1968.

Things began to turn around for the Indians in 1994, and they were 66-47 and in second place in the newly formed AL Central Division when the strike wiped out the rest of the year. It was the first of eight consecutive winning seasons for the franchise, highlighted by trips to the World Series in 1995 and 1997. They lost a six-game set to the Atlanta Braves in 1995, and the Florida Marlins won in seven games two years later.

The Indians have been in the playoffs four times since that heartbreaking defeat. The team lost in the ALCS in six games after the 1998 season, then dropped five-game ALDS tilts with the Red Sox in 1999 and the Seattle Mariners in 2001. Cleveland's last foray to the playoffs was 2007, when the Red Sox again ended the Indians' season with a seven-game victory in the ALCS.

The Indians have struggled since then, with a .500 record the best the team has to show for the 2008-2011 campaigns.

The Indians went from 68 victories in 2012 to 92 in 2013. The major improvement put them in second place in the AL Central, just one game behind the division-winning Tigers. Cleveland went to the AL Wild Card game but was blanked 4-0 by Tampa Bay to end their season. In 2014 Cleveland put together back-to-back winning seasons as they finished third in the AL Central with an 85-77 record. Corey Kluber had a terrific season as he went 18-9 with a 2.44 ERA and 269 strikeouts; he was named the AL Cy Young Award winner for his performance. The offseason has been a quiet one for the Tribe. Their biggest move was the acquisition of Brandon Moss from the Oakland A's in exchange for Joe Wendle. The team also inked Gavin Floyd to a one-year deal to add potential depth to their starting rotation.

Corey Kluber #28 of the Cleveland Indians in action against the New York Yankees at Yankee Stadium on August 9, 2014, in the Bronx borough of New York City. The Indians defeated the Yankees 3-0.

FIRST YEAR OF EXISTENCE: 1901
OWNER: LARRY DOLAN
MANAGER: TERRY FRANCONA (OCTOBER 6, 2012-PRESENT)

MAJOR LEAGUE TEAMS

COLORADO ROCKIES

The Colorado Rockies made their first appearance in Major League Baseball in 1993 as a NL West expansion team. They were one of two expansion teams introduced that season, the other being the then-Florida Marlins, who play in the NL East and are now known as the Miami Marlins. The franchise was awarded on July 5, 1991, and the team is named after the Rocky Mountains, which traverse through Colorado.

Colorado played their first major league game on April 5, 1993, losing 3-0 to the Mets. Colorado's first home game and first victory came on April 9, as they defeated the Montreal Expos 11-4. A crowd of 80,227, the largest to attend a regular season game in major league history, witnessed the game. The Rockies struggled as most expansion teams do, but did set a NL record for wins by an expansion team with 67. Additionally, the team set a major league record for attendance as 4,483,350 attended home games that season.

The Rockies broke the .500 mark for the first time early in the 1994 season, as the team was 6-5 following a win over the Expos on April 17. It was the only time they would be above .500 that season, finishing 53-64 and in last place in the NL West.

The team moved into Coors Field in 1995 and made their first playoff appearance that year after finishing with a 77-67 record. That mark was good for second in the NL West and earned them the wild card. The Rockies claimed their first postseason victory with a 7-5, 10-inning win in game three, but were eliminated in four games by the Atlanta Braves.

Colorado posted just three winning seasons between 1996 and 2006, finishing next to last or last in the division each time and never winning more than 83 games in a season. Larry Walker won the franchise's first Gold Glove and first MVP Award in 1997. Ellis Burks, Galarraga and Vinny Castilla each hit 40-plus home runs in 1996, and in 1997 Larry Walker, Castilla and Galaragga each slammed 40 or more homers.

The Rockies returned to the playoffs in 2007, when a furious September rally helped them come back from a six-game deficit to win the wild card. They won 14 of their final 15 games to set up a one-game playoff with the San Diego Padres. Colorado trailed 8-6 in the bottom of the 13th inning, but rallied with three runs in the bottom of the frame off Trevor Hoffman to claim a 9-8 victory and the wild card. Colorado swept the Philadelphia Phillies in the NLDS for their first postseason series victory and then defeated the Arizona Diamondbacks in the NLCS to make their first trip to the World Series.

Colorado seemed to have a world of momentum heading into the World Series against the Red Sox but, unfortunately for Colorado, the Red Sox walloped them 13-1 in Game One before taking the Series. Colorado returned to the playoffs in 2009, but was eliminated in the NLDS in four games.

The Rockies missed the playoffs for the fourth straight season in 2013 but improved by 10 games over 2012, finishing the year 74-88. Michael Cuddyer won the Silver Slugger Award as he hit .331 with 20 homers and 84 RBIs patrolling right field. He was one of four Rockies to hit at least 20 homers that season, joining Carlos Gonzalez (26), Troy Tulowitzki (25) and Wilin Rosario (21).

Colorado posted their fourth straight losing season as they finished 2014 with a 66-96 record. They simply couldn't hit away from Coors Field and it showed: Colorado hit .322 and slugged .529 while averaging 6.1 runs per game at home, while hitting just .229 and slugging .357 while averaging 3.1 runs a contest on the road. General Manager Dan O'Dowd resigned on October 8 and was replaced the same day by Jeff Bridich, who had been the director of the team's farm system.

The Rockies have had a fairly quiet offseason, with their biggest moves being the acquisitions of Daniel Descalso and Nick Hundley through free agency. Colorado is hoping for better years from Gonzalez and Tulowitzki, who are the anchors of their lineup.

Troy Tulowitzki #2 of the Colorado Rockies bats against the San Francisco Giants during the game at AT&T Park on Saturday, June 14, 2014, in San Francisco, CA.

FIRST YEAR OF EXISTENCE: 1993
OWNER: CHARLIE AND DICK MONFORT
MANAGER: WALT WEISS (NOVEMBER 7, 2012-PRESENT)

MAJOR LEAGUE TEAMS

DETROIT TIGERS

The Detroit Tigers have been a part of Major League Baseball since 1901, though the franchise dates back to 1894. Detroit has won 11 American League pennants and four World Series championships in franchise history. Additionally, 21 Hall of Fame inductees have worn a Tigers uniform.

The acquisition of Ty Cobb in 1905 helped lead the franchise to prominence, as the team already boasted Sam Crawford, Hughie Jennings, Bill Donovan and George Mullin and quickly got going with Cobb. Detroit claimed their first AL pennant in 1907 but was wiped out by the Chicago Cubs in four straight games in the World Series after a Game One tie. The Tigers won the AL pennant again in 1908 and were handcuffed by Cubs pitching, losing in five games. The Tigers won their third straight pennant in 1909 but were denied a championship as the Pittsburgh Pirates won Game Seven, 8-0.

Despite some tremendous efforts from the team, it was 25 years before they claimed another pennant. Cobb took over as player-manager from 1921 through 1926 but didn't lead Detroit to a pennant. The Tigers hit .316 in 1921, the highest team average in AL history, but finished 71-82.

The Tigers won the 1934 pennant but were unable to deliver in the World Series. They flopped in Game Seven as the Cardinals won 11-0 and took the title. The Tigers repeated as AL pennant winners in 1935 and knocked off the Cubs in six games to claim their first title.

Detroit returned to the World Series as the AL champions in 1940 but once again fell in Game Seven, losing to the Cincinnati Reds. Detroit exorcised the Game Seven demon in the 1945 World Series, beating the Cubs 9-3 for their second championship.

Detroit took their next pennant in 1968. Denny McLain won 31 games for the team, the last pitcher through 2014 to win 30 games in a season. The Tigers faced the Cardinals in the World Series with marquee pitching in McLain and Mickey Lolich. In the decisive Game Seven, Lolich outpitched Bob Gibson as the Tigers prevailed 4-1 and won the Series.

Detroit returned to the playoffs in 1972 as AL East champs but was defeated in the ALCS in five games by the Oakland A's. Detroit's next playoff appearance was 1984. The team swept the Kansas City Royals for the pennant and defeated the San Diego Padres in five games to claim the franchise's most recent title.

The Tigers won the AL East again in 1987 but were defeated by the Minnesota Twins four games to one. In 2006 Detroit beat the Yankees in four games in the ALDS and swept the Oakland A's in the ALCS to claim the pennant. The Tigers fell short in the World Series as the Cardinals won in five games.

Detroit returned to the playoffs in 2011, winning the AL Central. Justin Verlander claimed the AL Cy Young Award as well as the MVP Award. He was the first pitcher since Roger Clemens in 1986 to win MVP honors. The Tigers defeated the Yankees in five games in the ALDS but fell in six games to the Texas Rangers in the ALCS.

Miguel Cabrera won the Triple Crown in 2012 by hitting .330 with 44 homers and 139 RBIs; he also won the AL MVP. After winning the pennant in 2012 and getting swept by the San Francisco Giants in the World Series, the Tigers came back in 2013 focused. They won their third straight division crown as they went 93-69 in the regular season. Max Scherzer won the AL Cy Young Award while Cabrera won his third straight batting title and second straight AL MVP Award. The Tigers beat the A's in five games in the ALDS but lost in six games to Boston in the ALCS.

In 2014 the Tigers were 90-72 for their fourth straight AL Central title. Before the trade deadline, Detroit sent Drew Smyly and Willy Adames to Tampa Bay and Austin Jackson to Seattle in a three-team trade that saw them acquire David Price. The deal made the Tigers the first team in major league history to have three consecutive Cy Young Award winners in their rotation. All that pitching didn't help in the playoffs; they were swept by the Baltimore Orioles in the ALDS.

Victor Martinez #41 of the Detroit Tigers bats during the game against the Boston Red Sox at Comerica Park on June 6, 2014, in Detroit, MI. The Tigers defeated the Red Sox 6-2.

FIRST YEAR OF EXISTENCE: 1901
OWNER: MIKE ILITCH
MANAGER: BRAD AUSMUS (NOVEMBER 3, 2013-PRESENT)

MAJOR LEAGUE TEAMS

HOUSTON ASTROS

The Houston Astros franchise made its presence known in Major League Baseball when the National League expanded in 1962. The Astros, then known as the Colt .45s, were one of two expansion teams; the other was the New York Mets. The club changed its name to the Astros prior to the 1965 season to coincide with the building of the first multipurpose domed stadium in history, which was christened the Astrodome.

The franchise played the first game in its history on April 10, 1962, drubbing the Chicago Cubs 11-2 in front of 25,271 at Colt Stadium. The momentum failed to last and the Astros came crashing back to earth, finishing 64-96. That record was good enough for eighth in the 10-team NL and 24 games better than their expansion brethren Mets.

The Astros lost at least 90 games in each of their first seven seasons in the majors, finally breaking the trend with an 81-81 season in 1969. The team helped sculpt the NL landscape with a 1971 trade with the Cincinnati Reds. Houston dealt Joe Morgan, Denis Menke, Jack Billingham, Cesar Geronimo and Ed Armbrister to the Reds for Lee May, Tommy Helms and Jimmy Stewart. The Astros were tied for second in 1972 with a record of 84-69 but that win total would be the franchise's high-water mark until 1979 when they won 89 games.

The Astros made the playoffs for the first time in franchise history in 1980 after winning a one-game playoff with the Los Angeles Dodgers to claim the NL West title, but they lost in five games to the Philadelphia Phillies in the NL Championship Series. Houston returned to the playoffs in the strike-interrupted 1981 season but was defeated in four games by the Los Angeles Dodgers in the Division Series. Houston claimed their third division crown in 1986 with Mike Scott and Nolan Ryan at the front of the rotation but once again was denied a trip to the World Series. They fell to the Mets in six games in the NLCS.

In 1997 Houston claimed the first of three straight NL Central Division championships, but they were swept by the Atlanta Braves in the NLDS. The team won a franchise-record 102 games in 1998 but failed to get past the Division Series, losing to the Padres in four games. The 1999 season saw Houston eliminated in four games in the Division Series by Atlanta. The Braves also knocked Houston out in three games in 2001.

The Astros took a step forward in 2004. After winning the NL wild card with 92 victories, they claimed their first playoff series win, defeating their nemesis, the Braves, in five games. In the NLCS, Houston led three games to two but was unable to close the deal, and the Cardinals took the last two games and the pennant.

The Astros made their first and, to date, only World Series appearance in 2005. The team claimed the NL wild card and then beat the Braves in four games in the NLDS, setting up a rematch in the NLCS with the Cardinals. Houston defeated the Cardinals in six games to reach to the World Series. The team simply ran out of steam in the World Series, however, and the White Sox swept them in four straight games.

The Astros have posted just two winning seasons and no playoff appearances in the last nine seasons through 2014, including a franchise-record 111 losses in 2013. Houston became the first team in major league history to have the first overall pick in the draft three seasons in a row. The Astros improved 19 games in the standings in 2014 as they finished the year 70-92. Bo Porter was fired as manager on September 1. Meanwhile, Jose Altuve won the American League batting title as he finished the year with a .341 mark and 225 hits.

After the season came to a close, A. J. Hinch was named the team's manager. In an effort to add pieces to their lineup in 2015, the Astros were active in free agency: they added shortstop Jed Lowrie on a three-year deal and relievers Luke Gregerson and Pat Neshek on three- and two-year deals. The Astros also acquired catcher Hank Conger in a deal with the Angels for Nick Tropeano and Carlos Perez.

Craig Biggio #7 of the Houston Astros in position during a baseball game against the San Francisco Giants on August 6, 1993, at Candlestick Park in San Francisco, CA. The Giants won 6-4.

FIRST YEAR OF EXISTENCE: 1962
OWNER: JIM CRANE
MANAGER: A.J. HINCH (SEPTEMBER 29, 2014-PRESENT)

MAJOR LEAGUE TEAMS

KANSAS CITY ROYALS

The Kansas City Royals made their debut in Major League Baseball in 1969. The Royals joined the major leagues along with the Montreal Expos and San Diego Padres in the National League and the Seattle Pilots in the American League. The team has had its ups and down and has claimed three pennants and one World Series championship in franchise history.

The Royals came into existence as a replacement for the Kansas City A's, who moved to Oakland after the 1967 season. The team played the first game in franchise history on April 8, 1969, against the Minnesota Twins; the Royals won, 4-3, in 12 innings. The team finished with a record of 69-93 on the year, and Lou Piniella won the AL Rookie of the Year Award in the franchise's first year.

The Royals had their first winning season in 1971 with an 85-76 record. Kansas City broke through for their first division crown and playoff appearance in 1976. They won 90 games but were bested three games to two in the ALCS by the New York Yankees. It was the start of a successful decade for the Royals: from 1976 to 1985, Kansas City made the playoffs seven times. The Royals lost in the ALCS in 1977 to the Yankees in five games after the team recorded a franchise-record 102 victories that year. The 1978 season saw Kansas City's third straight division crown, but the Royals were knocked off by the Yankees in four games. The Royals claimed their fourth division crown in five seasons in 1980 and won the first playoff series in team history, sweeping the Yankees to make the World Series for the first time. Kansas City was defeated in six games in the World Series by the Philadelphia Phillies.

Due to the strike interrupting the 1981 season, baseball's season was split into two halves. The Royals won the first half of the season but actually finished the year with a losing record. They were swept by the A's in the AL Division Series, scoring just two runs in the process. The Royals returned to the playoffs in 1984 but lost to the Detroit Tigers in three straight games.

In 1985 the Royals claimed the AL West title. The team rallied from a three-games-to-one deficit to stun the Toronto Blue Jays in the ALCS and make the World Series for the second time. The Royals once again fell behind three games to one, this time to St. Louis, but rallied again. The key play came in Game Six, when in the ninth inning, trailing 1-0, Jorge Orta was called safe on a controversial call by umpire Don Denkinger. Later in the inning a misplayed pop up and a passed ball helped the Royals, and Dane Iorg's pinch-hit single won the game for Kansas City. In Game Seven, Bret Saberhagen shut down the Cardinals, and a six-run fifth inning sealed the victory. Kansas City won Game Seven 11-0 and claimed the team's first and, through 2014, only championship.

The Royals had three straight winning seasons from 1987 to 1989, finishing no higher than second in the AL West. From 1993 to 2013, they posted just two winning seasons and were better than third in the division only once. The Royals posted their best record since 1989 in 2013, putting together an 86-76 record on the season.

Kansas City snapped a 28-season playoff drought as they qualified for the first time since winning the World Series in 1985. The team finished 89-73 to earn a wild-card berth. They trailed the Oakland A's 7-3 in the eighth inning but then rallied to send the game to extra innings. After Oakland regained the lead in the top of the 12th, Kansas City scored twice in the bottom of the frame, winning 9-8 on Salvador Perez's walk-off single.

The Royals swept the Los Angeles Angels of Anaheim in the ALDS and then swept the Baltimore Orioles in the ALCS; their eight-game win streak to start a postseason was a major league record. In the World Series, the Royals took the Giants to the limit. In the decisive seventh game, the Royals had the tying run in scoring position in the ninth inning but couldn't push it across, giving the Giants their third title in five years.

Eric Hosmer #35 of the Kansas City Royals hits a single in the third inning to score Lorenzo Cain #6 against Bud Norris #25 of the Baltimore Orioles during Game Two of the American League Championship Series at Oriole Park at Camden Yards on October 11, 2014, in Baltimore, MA.

FIRST YEAR OF EXISTENCE: 1969
OWNER: DAVID GLASS
MANAGER: NED YOST (MAY 13, 2010-PRESENT)

MAJOR LEAGUE TEAMS

LOS ANGELES ANGELS OF ANAHEIM

The Los Angeles Angels of Anaheim were part of a vigorous expansion plan by Major League Baseball to the West Coast in 1961. At that time, the team was known as the Los Angeles Angels, which was their name until they became the California Angels on September 2, 1965. After the 1996 season, they became the Anaheim Angels with their current name taking effect in 2005. The team has won just one World Series, that coming with their only American League pennant back in 2002.

The Angels made their major league debut on April 11, 1961, in Baltimore against the Orioles and took a 7-2 win. They finished the season 70-91, good for eighth place in the 10-team American League. The Angels put together their first winning season in their second year, going 86-76 and finishing third. That proved to be their high-water mark until they won 87 in 1978.

The Angels claimed their first division championship and made their first playoff appearance in 1979. Their foray into the postseason was short lived, as the Orioles knocked them out in the ALCS in four games. Jim Fregosi, who was the team's manager for that 1979 run, was fired partway through 1981 and was replaced by Gene Mauch, who would be the manager through most of the Angels' good years in the 1980s.

The 1982 season saw the Angels rack up 93 victories in the regular season en route to the AL West championship. The team was thwarted by the Milwaukee Brewers, who won the AL pennant with a five-game series win in the ALCS. The Angels would return to the ALCS in 1986 and led Boston three games to one, but things fell apart for them from there.

Leading 5-2 in the ninth inning of Game Five, Mike Witt gave up a two-run home run to Don Baylor to cut the lead to 5-4. Reliever Gary Lucas hit catcher Rich Gedman with his only pitch of the game and Dave Henderson blasted a two-run, two-out, two-strike home run off Donnie Moore to give Boston a 6-5 lead. The Angels tied the game in the bottom of the ninth but Henderson's sacrifice fly in the 11th gave Boston a 7-6 win.

The Angels were clobbered in Games Six and Seven in Boston and it was the Red Sox who went on to the World Series. The Angels would not see the playoffs again until 2002.

In 2002 the Angels' 99 victories were only good for the AL wild card, as the Oakland A's won the division with 103 wins. The Angels claimed their first postseason series victory by beating the Yankees in four games; the Angels beat the Twins in five games to claim their first AL pennant. The Angels lost Game One of the World Series to the San Francisco Giants, won the next two and then dropped two straight to fall behind three games to two.

In Game Six, the Angels were down 5-0 in the seventh inning and just eight outs away from elimination. The team rallied for a 6-5 victory, sending the series to a seventh game, which they won 4-1 as John Lackey became the first rookie pitcher to win Game Seven of the World Series since Babe Adams in 1909. Through the 2014 season, this marked the only appearance in the World Series for the franchise.

The Angels made the playoffs in 2004, 2005, 2007, 2008 and 2009 but were not terribly successful, winning just two playoff series in that six-year span. They made a major splash in free agency in the 2011 offseason, signing C.J. Wilson and Albert Pujols. After missing the postseason in 2012 following their big offseason moves, the Angels made another bold move as they acquired Josh Hamilton as a free agent. The problem was the same: the Angels finished 2013 78-84, 18 games off the pace in the AL West.

The Angels snapped a four-year playoff drought as they took advantage of Oakland's freefall in the second half of the 2014 season to win the AL West with a 98-64 record. The playoffs didn't go the Angels' way, though, and they were swept by the Kansas City Royals in the ALDS. Outfielder Mike Trout won his first AL MVP Award as he hit .287 with 39 doubles, 9 triples, 36 home runs, 111 RBIs, 16 steals and 115 runs scored.

Albert Pujols #5 of the Los Angeles Angels of Anaheim hits a solo home run in the third inning against the Oakland Athletics at Angel Stadium of Anaheim on April 14, 2014, in Anaheim, California. It was Pujols' 496th career home run.

FIRST YEAR OF EXISTENCE: 1961
OWNER: ARTE MORENO
MANAGER: MIKE SCIOSCIA (NOVEMBER 18, 1999-PRESENT)

MAJOR LEAGUE TEAMS

LOS ANGELES DODGERS

The Los Angeles Dodgers franchise is one of the oldest in Major League Baseball, having played its first game in 1884 in the American Association. The team has had a variety of different monikers but settled on the Dodgers in 1932, with the only change since being the move from Brooklyn to Los Angeles in 1958.

The Dodgers began play in the National League after six years in the American Association. The club, then known as the Bridegrooms, played its first NL game on April 19, 1890, losing 15-9 to the Boston Beaneaters. The Bridegrooms claimed the NL pennant that year, finishing 86-43. The team claimed the 1899 NL pennant after winning 101 games.

The team's first pennant in the World Series era came in 1916 after winning 94 games in the regular season. They didn't fare as well in the postseason, losing to the Red Sox in five games. The team would return to the World Series in 1920 but were defeated by the Cleveland Indians, five games to two.

The Dodgers didn't win another pennant until 1941, and they fell in five games to the New York Yankees in the World Series. The 1942 team won a franchise-record 104 games but failed to win the pennant, finishing second behind the St. Louis Cardinals.

The Dodgers broke the major league color barrier in 1947 when Jackie Robinson made his debut for the team. Robinson was the first black player in history; with him in the lineup, the Dodgers claimed the pennant but fell short in the World Series.

In what became a common matchup over the next decade, the Yankees beat the Dodgers in seven games. The teams clashed again in 1949, with the Yankees prevailing in five games to deny Brooklyn their first championship.

The Dodgers claimed pennants in 1952 and 1953 but lost the World Series both years to the Yankees. The Dodgers finally got their first championship in 1955, besting the Yankees in seven games. The two teams met again in 1956 and the Yankees prevailed with help from Don Larsen's perfect game.

The team moved from Brooklyn to Los Angeles in 1958, and in 1959 the team had another pennant. The Dodgers beat the Chicago White Sox in the World Series to win their second title. The Dodgers swept the Yankees in the 1963 World Series and defeated the Minnesota Twins in 1965. They claimed the pennant in 1966 but were swept by the Orioles and didn't return to the playoffs until 1974. The Dodgers beat the Pirates in the NLCS before losing to the Oakland A's in the World Series.

The Dodgers won the NL pennant again in 1977 and 1978, but they lost to the Yankees both times. The two teams met again in the World Series during the strike-shortened 1981 season and the Dodgers won in six games. The Dodgers lost in the NLCS in 1983 and 1985 before returning to the World Series in 1988. They won their most recent title with a five-game series win over the A's.

Frank McCourt sold the team on March 27, 2012, to the Guggenheim Baseball Management Group that included NBA Hall of Famer Magic Johnson for a staggering $2 billion. The ownership change didn't pay immediate dividends as the Dodgers finished 86-76 and missed the postseason.

In 2013 the Dodgers were floundering in early June, sitting 23-32 and in last place in the NL West, 8.5 games out of the division lead. The team called up Yasiel Puig and the Dodgers went 69-38 the rest of the way to win the division by 11 games. Los Angeles knocked off Atlanta three games to one in the NL Division Series before falling four games to two to the Cardinals in the NLCS.

In the offseason, Kershaw signed a seven-year extension through the 2020 season worth $215 million. Los Angeles won their second straight NL West crown in 2014 as they finished the regular season with a record of 94-68. Kershaw won his third Cy Young Award, becoming the first NL pitcher since Bob Gibson in 1967 to claim the NL MVP Award. Despite their regular season success, the Dodgers flopped in the postseason, falling in four games to the Cardinals in the NLDS.

Adrian Gonzalez #23 of the Los Angeles Dodgers takes the throw at first base during the game against the St. Louis Cardinals at Busch Stadium on July 19, 2014, in St. Louis, MO. The Cardinals won the game 4-2.

FIRST YEAR OF EXISTENCE: 1884
OWNER: GUGGENHEIM BASEBALL MANAGEMENT
MANAGER: DON MATTINGLY (SEPTEMBER 18, 2010-PRESENT)

MAJOR LEAGUE TEAMS

MIAMI MARLINS

The Miami Marlins began their existence in Major League Baseball in 1993 as the Florida Marlins. They were one of two expansion teams introduced that season, with the other being the Colorado Rockies. Both teams were placed in the National League, with the Marlins in the NL East and the Rockies in the NL West. With a new stadium opening in 2012, the Marlins changed their name from the Florida Marlins to the Miami Marlins.

The Marlins played the first game in franchise history on April 5, 1993, before a home crowd of 42,334. The team defeated the Los Angeles Dodgers 6-3, as knuckleballer Charlie Hough got the win. Gary Sheffield and closer Bryan Harvey would be the Marlins' first All-Star selections and the team finished 64-98.

The team's winning percentage improved over the coming seasons, as Florida finished 51-62 in the strike-shortened 1994 season and were 67-76 in 1995. Perhaps the biggest move the Marlins made after the 1996 season was not on the field, but in the dugout: the team hired Jim Leyland to take over as manager.

The Marlins seemed to put it all together in 1997 as they posted the first winning record in franchise history by going 92-70. That record was good enough to claim the wild card in the NL, giving the Marlins the first playoff berth in franchise history. They swept the San Francisco Giants in the NLDS for their first playoff series victory.

That set the Marlins up with the NL East champion Atlanta Braves in the NLCS. The Marlins knocked off the favored Braves in six games to claim their first NL pennant and advanced to the World Series against the Cleveland Indians. The Marlins and Indians split the first six games, sending it to a winner-take-all Game Seven. Cleveland took a 2-1 lead into the bottom of the ninth inning but Craig Counsell tied the game with a sacrifice fly. In the bottom of the 11th, Edgar Renteria's walk-off single gave the Marlins a 3-2 win and the World Series.

Immediately following that victory, ownership destroyed the team in a fire sale. The Marlins flopped to 54-108 and are the only team in major league history to win a World Series one year and lose 100 games the next.

The Marlins returned to prominence in 2003, as the club made the playoffs as the wild card. They handled the Giants in the divisional round this time, and then staged a comeback from a 3-games-to-1 deficit in the NLCS against the Chicago Cubs. Steve Bartman's interference on a foul ball hit by Luis Castillo helped open the floodgates to an eight-run inning in Game Six. The Marlins rallied from a deficit in Game Seven against Kerry Wood to claim an improbable pennant. The team's success continued in the World Series as the Marlins bested the Yankees in six games to claim their second title.

The Marlins have not returned to the playoffs since their second championship. They finished the 2011 season in last place in the NL East with a record of 72-90. Intent on changing the complexion of the club with a new stadium, ownership hired Ozzie Guillen as manager while adding pitchers Mark Buehrle and Carlos Zambrano, along with shortstop Jose Reyes, in an effort to bolster the talent base.

The Guillen experiment proved to be a disaster as the Marlins went 69-93 in the 2012 season. Guillen was a lightning rod for controversy and ended up being fired when the season was over.

The 2013 season was another rocky one as they finished their first year under Mike Redmond 62-100. One bright spot for Miami was the emergence of starting pitcher Jose Fernandez, who went 12-6 with a 2.19 ERA in 28 starts while fanning 187 hitters; he was named the NL Rookie of the Year.

Miami finished the 2014 season with a 77-85 record, which was better than expected after Jose Fernandez went down with Tommy John surgery partway through the season. In a change of attitude, the Marlins inked Giancarlo Stanton to a 13-year extension of his contract worth $325 million though he can opt out of the deal at age 30.

Pitcher Henderson Alvarez #37 of the Miami Marlins throws a pitch in the bottom of the first inning against the Miami Marlins on September 12, 2014, at Citizens Bank Park in Philadelphia, PA.

MARLINS
FIRST YEAR OF EXISTENCE: 1993
OWNER: JEFFREY LORIA
MANAGER: MIKE REDMOND (NOVEMBER 1, 2012-PRESENT)

MAJOR LEAGUE TEAMS

MILWAUKEE BREWERS

The Milwaukee Brewers were part of Major League Baseball's four-team expansion class of 1969. This expansion took place as the league transitioned to having two divisions in each league. The Montreal Expos and San Diego Padres joined the National League, while the Kansas City Royals joined the American League at the same time as the Brewers, who were known as the Seattle Pilots. The Brewers franchise has yet to claim a World Series championship and have just one AL pennant to their credit.

The franchise made its major league debut April 8, 1969, on the road against the California Angels. The team was victorious by a score of 4-3. That was one of the high points of the season for the Pilots, who ended up the season 64-98 and in the cellar of the AL West. As it would turn out, the Pilots' first season in Seattle would be their last.

The team moved to Milwaukee in time for the 1970 season after Marvin Miles took the stand in a hearing held in the King County courthouse. Miles told the judge that he was unable to pay the salaries of the office staff, coaches and scouts. He also lacked the funding to pay the bonuses that were due to players, while meeting payroll was a serious issue. Should payroll be met 10 days late, all the contracts would be declared void, the players would become free agents, and the team as it was known would cease to exist. After this testimony, the restriction holding the team to Seattle was lifted.

The team became known as the Milwaukee Brewers, but even with the name and location change, the product on the field did not improve for several years. Milwaukee posted their first winning season in 1978 with a 93-victory campaign but finished just third in the division. That was the first of six straight winning seasons through 1983 for the club. Milwaukee made their first playoff appearance in the strike-shortened 1981 season but was defeated by the New York Yankees in four games in the Division Series; Rollie Fingers won the AL MVP and Cy Young Award.

The Brewers won the 1982 AL East title with a 95-67 record. Don Sutton, who the Brewers acquired on August 30, outpitched Jim Palmer of the Baltimore Orioles in the season finale and Robin Yount's two home runs led the Brewers to the division crown. The Brewers edged the California Angels, three games to two, in the ALCS to claim their first and, through 2014, only pennant in franchise history. The Brewers led the World Series three games to two over the St. Louis Cardinals but dropped Games Six and Seven. The Game Seven defeat denied the Brewers their first World Series championship, something they still are seeking as of 2014.

The 1982 World Series marked the last playoff appearance for the Brewers until the 2008 season. In between, they switched leagues and divisions to the NL Central and saw the league expand on multiple occasions. The team made the 2008 playoffs as a wild card thanks to the acquisition of CC Sabathia near the trade deadline, but the Phillies dispatched the Brewers in four games in the NLDS.

The Brewers won their first NL Central title in 2011. The club won a franchise-record 96 games during the regular season and edged the Arizona Diamondbacks in five games during the NLDS. That put the Brewers in the NLCS against the St. Louis Cardinals. They were defeated in six games in the NLCS, ending their season. Ryan Braun won the NL MVP for his performance.

The 2013 season was a lost cause on many fronts for the Brewers as they ended up 74-88 and in fourth place in the NL Central, 23 games behind the division leading Cardinals. Yovani Gallardo led the Brewers with 12 wins. In an effort to beef up the rotation, Milwaukee signed Matt Garza to a four-year deal worth $52 million in the offseason. Milwaukee was in the driver's seat in the NL Central for most of the year but faded down the stretch and ended with an 82-80 record, leaving them in third place in the division, eight games off the pace and out of the playoffs.

Carlos Gomez #27 of the Milwaukee Brewers bats against the Washington Nationals at Nationals Park on July 20, 2014, in Washington, DC.

FIRST YEAR OF EXISTENCE: 1969
OWNER: MARK ATTANASIO
MANAGER: RON ROENICKE (NOVEMBER 2, 2010-PRESENT)

MAJOR LEAGUE TEAMS

MINNESOTA TWINS

The Minnesota Twins franchise has existed since 1894 when it was part of what was then known as the Western League. The team was known as the Washington Senators and didn't move to Minneapolis and become the Twins until 1961. The franchise has three World Series championships and six AL pennants to its credit.

The Senators played their first season in the AL in 1901. They struggled to a 61-72 record, playing so poorly that San Francisco Chronicle columnist Charlie Dryden came up with a quip that followed the franchise: "Washington: First in war, first in peace, and last in the American League."

The Senators' fortunes began to turn after the 1907 discovery of pitcher Walter Johnson, who would win 417 games in his career, the second most all time. The team posted their first winning season in 1912 as they won 91 games.

The Senators claimed their first AL pennant in 1924 after winning 92 games. They bested the Yankees to win the pennant and made their first World Series appearance. Their opponents were the New York Giants, managed by future Hall of Fame manager John McGraw.

In a tie game in the ninth inning of Game Seven, Senators player-manager Bucky Harris brought Johnson in out of the bullpen on one day's rest. Johnson threw four scoreless frames, and in the 12th inning a ball bounced over Giants third baseman Freddie Lindstrom and into left field. Muddy Ruel scored the winning run and the Senators had their first championship. The team captured their second consecutive AL pennant in 1925 but the Pirates won the World Series, four games to three.

In 1933 Washington won the pennant along with 99 regular season games. They were unable to win the championship, losing to the Giants in five games. It was the last pennant that the franchise won in Washington.

The club would relocate from Washington to Minnesota after the 1960 season, based on the provision that a new expansion team would be placed in the city and keep the Senators name.

The relocated Senators became the Minnesota Twins. The Twins made the World Series in 1965 as they won their first pennant in Minnesota, but they lost in seven games to the Los Angeles Dodgers. The loss stung the Twins, who won a franchise-record 102 games. They won the AL West in 1969 and 1970 but lost in the ALCS.

The Twins did not make the postseason again until 1987 when they won the AL West. They beat the Detroit Tigers in five games to win the pennant and set up a matchup with the St. Louis Cardinals in the World Series. The series went to seven games, with the Twins' 4-2 victory in Game Seven giving them their second championship.

The Twins claimed their second World Series crown in Minnesota and third in franchise history in 1991. Minnesota claimed the AL West and defeated the Toronto Blue Jays in five games to win the AL pennant. The Twins beat the Atlanta Braves in seven games after Kirby Puckett hit a walk-off home run in Game Six to even the series. In Game Seven, Jack Morris threw 10 shutout innings as the Twins won by a score of 1-0 to take the title.

From 2001 through 2014, the Twins made the playoffs six times but won just once. They were defeated in the ALCS in 2002 and lost in the divisional round in 2003, 2004, 2006, 2009 and 2010. They fell on hard times in 2011, finishing with a record of just 63-99 due to injuries to stars Joe Mauer and Justin Morneau. The 2012 season wasn't any better as Minnesota went 66-96 and finished at the bottom of the AL Central for the second straight season.

In 2013 the Twins failed to make progress as far as improving their win total as they again went 66-96. They did improve to fourth place in the AL Central, mainly due to the ineptitude and bungling of the White Sox. Minnesota finished the 2014 season with a 70-92 record, which was four games better than 2013 but wasn't enough to save Ron Gardenhire's job. On November 3, the team named Paul Molitor the new manager of the franchise.

First baseman Joe Mauer #7 of the Minnesota Twins fields his position as he dives to make the catch of a hard hit ground ball in the game against the Kansas City Royals on April 20, 2014, at Kauffman Stadium in Kansas City, MO.

FIRST YEAR OF EXISTENCE: 1894
OWNER: JIM POHLAD
MANAGER: PAUL MOLITOR (NOVEMBER 3, 2014-PRESENT)

MAJOR LEAGUE TEAMS

NEW YORK METS

The New York Mets have been a part of the Major League Baseball scene since 1962 as part of a two-team expansion in the National League along with the Houston Colt .45s, now known as the Houston Astros. The Mets have claimed four NL pennants and two World Series championships in franchise history.

The Mets played their first game on April 11, 1962, in St. Louis against the Cardinals. The team finished with a record of 40-120, the worst record in major league history since the schedule expanded to 162 games. They lost at least 100 games in five of their first six seasons, with a 95-loss campaign in 1966 their best season.

That all changed, seemingly in the blink of an eye, in 1969. The Mets got hot the last two months of the season, making up a 10-game deficit from mid-August on to claim the NL East. The team won 100 games led by Tom Seaver's 25 victories. In their first NLCS, the Mets swept the Atlanta Braves. That set up a World Series matchup with the Baltimore Orioles; the Mets shocked the Orioles with a five-game victory to claim their first championship.

In 1973 the Mets were just 82-79 but won the NL East. In the playoffs, they stunned the Cincinnati Reds three games to two in the NLCS to win their second pennant, but they ran into a tough Oakland A's club in the World Series and blew a 3-2 lead, losing in seven games.

The Mets broke through in 1986, winning the NL East with a league-best 108 victories. They beat the Astros in the NLCS in six games to clinch the flag. The Mets faced the Red Sox in the World Series and trailed by two runs in the bottom of the 10th inning of Game Six.

The Mets were behind 3-2 in the series and after the first two hitters were retired, they were down to their final out. Mookie Wilson's grounder up the first base line eluded Bill Buckner's glove, capping a three-run rally and the Mets stunned Boston. They took Game Seven and won the World Series, their most recent championship in franchise history.

In 1988 the Mets won 100 games and the NL East crown. In the playoffs, the Dodgers, led by Orel Hershisher in Game Seven, managed to beat the Mets and win the pennant. The team would not return to postseason play until 1999, when they beat the Cincinnati Reds in a one-game playoff for the wild card. They beat the Arizona Diamondbacks in four games in the NLDS before falling to the Braves in six games of the NLCS.

The Mets were the NL wild card in 2000 and beat the San Francisco Giants three games to one in the NLDS to set up a matchup with the Cardinals in the NLCS. The Mets prevailed in five games in the NLCS, setting up a World Series matchup with their crosstown rivals, the Yankees. The Mets were not successful in the "Subway Series," as the Yankees beat the Mets in five games. The 2000 season marks the most recent World Series trip for the Mets as of 2014. They have been to the playoffs just once since 2000, winning the NL East in 2006. The Mets swept the Dodgers in the NLDS but lost to the Cardinals in seven games in the NLCS. The Mets finished 77-85 in 2011, their third consecutive losing season.

The Mets struggled in 2012 as they finished the year 74-88 and in fourth place in the NL East. The season's high point was Johan Santana's no-hitter on June 1 against the Cardinals. Santana was on a pitch count of 110 pitches following shoulder surgery; he threw 134 in that contest. It was the first no-hitter in franchise history. In 2013 the Mets posted a 74-88 mark though they moved up to third in the NL East. Matt Harvey, the ace of the rotation, was in the All-Star Game and went 9-5 on the year but had to undergo Tommy John surgery and missed the entire 2014 season.

The Mets improved to 79-83 in 2014 and finished in a second-place tie with the Braves in the NL East but failed to finish above .500 for the sixth straight year. They did get a solid performance from Jacob deGrom, who finished 9-6 with a 2.69 ERA in 22 starts; he was named NL Rookie of the Year.

New York Mets catcher Mike Piazza (L) tags out Philadelphia Phillies second baseman Mark Lewis after he tried to score from second base on a single in the top of the second inning 19 July at Shea Stadium in New York City.

FIRST YEAR OF EXISTENCE: 1962
OWNER: FRED WILPON (MAJORITY OWNER)
MANAGER: TERRY COLLINS (NOVEMBER 23, 2010-PRESENT)

MAJOR LEAGUE TEAMS

NEW YORK YANKEES

The New York Yankees have been a part of the AL since its inception as a major league in 1901. The Yankees are the most successful franchise in major league history, capturing 40 AL pennants and 27 World Series championships.

The Yankees began their existence in 1901 as the Baltimore Orioles. After a disappointing 1902 season, the two major leagues agreed to put a team in New York to play alongside the New York Giants. The Orioles moved to New York and became the New York Highlanders, changing their name to the Yankees in 1913.

The Red Sox sold Babe Ruth to the Yankees after the 1919 season as Harry Frazee was trying to accumulate cash resources. Ruth would go on to be a star for New York, while Boston didn't win a World Series championship for 86 years.

With Ruth in the lineup, the Yankees claimed their first pennant in 1921 but lost to the crosstown Giants, five games to three in the World Series. The Yankees claimed pennants in 1922 and 1923: the team was swept in 1922 by the Giants but won their first World Series championship in 1923 over the Giants.

The Yankees took pennants in 1926, 1927, and 1928, losing to the Cardinals in the 1926 World Series but winning the 1927 and 1928 Series by sweeping the Pittsburgh Pirates and Cardinals.

The last Ruth-era AL pennant the Yankees claimed came in 1932. The Yankees swept the Chicago Cubs to win the title, highlighted by Ruth's "called shot" in Game Three off Charlie Root.

The Yankees won four straight titles between 1936 and 1939, beating the Giants in 1936 and 1937, the Cubs in 1938 and the Reds in 1939. The 1941 World Series marked the first clash between the Dodgers and Yankees, with New York taking the Series in five games. St. Louis beat the Yankees in five games in 1942 but the Yankees beat the Cardinals in five games in 1943.

The Yankees won the pennant in 1947 and beat the Dodgers in the World Series. The Yankees won five straight titles from 1949 to 1953. The Dodgers were the victims in 1949, 1952 and 1953, while the Philadelphia Phillies fell in 1950 and the Giants in 1951. The Dodgers defeated the Yankees in the 1955 World Series but New York struck back in 1956. The Yankees lost to the Milwaukee Braves in 1957 World Series before beating them in the 1958 Series.

The Yankees won the AL flag again in 1960 but lost to the Pirates on Bill Mazeroski's walk-off series-ending home run in the bottom of the ninth inning of Game Seven. It was the first of five straight pennants for the Yankees through 1964, however they lost three of the five World Series. New York lost in 1960 to Pittsburgh, in 1963 to the Dodgers and in 1964 to the Cardinals. They beat the Reds in 1961 and the Giants in 1962.

New York took three straight pennants from 1976 to 1978, winning two World Series. They were swept in the 1976 Series by the Big Red Machine before beating the Dodgers for the 1977 and 1978 titles. The Yankees lost in the ALCS by the Royals in 1980 and dropped the 1981 World Series to the Dodgers in six games.

New York made the postseason in 16 of 17 seasons between 1995 and 2011, winning five World Series championships, including three in a row, from 1998 to 2000. In addition, the team won titles in 1996 and 2009 while losing in the 2001 and 2003 World Series to the Arizona Diamondbacks and Florida Marlins, respectively. The Yankees were defeated in the ALDS, three games to two, by the Detroit Tigers in 2011. Derek Jeter collected his 3000th career hit in 2011 with a home run against Tampa Bay on July 9.

The Yankees made the playoffs in 2012 as they won 95 games and reached the ALCS before being swept by the Tigers. The 2013 season was one of disappointment for the Yankees as they finished 85-77 and in third place in the AL East, missing the playoffs. New York finished the 2014 campaign with an 84-78 record and in second place in the AL East and missed the playoffs. The season was Derek Jeter's swan song and the Yankees couldn't deliver him a playoff berth.

Mariano Rivera #42 of the New York Yankees pitches against the Oakland Athletics on April 21, 2009, at Yankee Stadium in the Bronx borough of New York City.

FIRST YEAR OF EXISTENCE: 1901
OWNER: YANKEE GLOBAL ENTERPRISES, LLC
MANAGER: JOE GIRARDI (OCTOBER 30, 2007-PRESENT)

MAJOR LEAGUE TEAMS

OAKLAND ATHLETICS

The Oakland Athletics have been a part of Major League Baseball since 1901, when they were one of the eight charter members of the American League. The franchise began in Philadelphia as the Philadelphia Athletics under Connie Mack and moved to Kansas City in 1955 before finally relocating to Oakland in time for the 1968 season. The franchise has nine World Series championships and 15 AL pennants to its credit.

Connie Mack was a staple of the A's franchise, having managed the team each year from 1901 through 1950. The franchise played their first major league game on April 26, 1901, and lost to the Washington Senators 5-1. The A's finished the 1901 season with a mark of 74-62, and in 1902 the team won its first pennant in franchise history, going 83-53.

The Athletics made their first appearance in the World Series after winning the 1905 AL pennant. The club faced the New York Giants and lost the series in five games. The A's didn't claim another pennant until 1910. They won their first World Series title that year, defeating the Chicago Cubs in five games. The A's defended their title in 1911, beating the Giants in six games. They also won pennants in 1913 and 1914, which gave them four pennants in five seasons. Philadelphia won their third World Series title in four years in 1913 with a five-game victory over the Giants but was swept in the 1914 World Series by the Boston Braves.

The team claimed three consecutive pennants between 1929 and 1931. They won the 1929 World Series in five games over the Cubs and won the 1930 Series over the St. Louis Cardinals before losing to the Cardinals in the 1931 Series.

The franchise next made the playoffs in 1971 in Oakland after winning the AL West but was swept by Baltimore. Oakland won AL pennants in 1972, 1973 and 1974, winning the World Series in each of those years: they defeated Cincinnati in 1972, the New York Mets in 1973 and the Los Angeles Dodgers in 1974. The team won the division in 1975 but was beaten by the Boston Red Sox in the ALCS.

The Athletics returned to the playoffs in 1981 but lost in the ALCS in the strike-shortened season to the New York Yankees. The team won three straight pennants from 1988 through 1990 but won just one World Series. After losing in five games to the Dodgers in 1988, the team swept the San Francisco Giants in 1989 in a series delayed by an earthquake. The Reds swept the A's in 1990, marking the franchise's most recent trip to the Fall Classic as of 2014.

Oakland was defeated in the ALCS by Toronto in 1992. Oakland appeared in the playoffs four straight years from 2000 through 2003 but was dropped in the ALDS on each occasion. In 2006 Oakland swept the Minnesota Twins in the divisional round before falling to the Detroit Tigers in the ALCS.

The team went 74-88 in 2011 and dealt arguably their best starting pitcher, Gio Gonzalez, to the Washington Nationals in exchange for four prospects. The 2012 A's went on to win 94 games and their first division title since 2006; they were knocked off in five games by the Tigers in the ALDS. Oakland had a successful 2013 season as they defended their division crown. The A's won 96 games but for the second consecutive season, things didn't go Oakland's way in the playoffs. They were upended in five games with the Tigers proving to be their foil once again.

Oakland finished the 2014 season with an 88-74 record and ended up second in the AL West, 10 games behind the Angels in the standings. Several deals were made during the year to bolster the team for a postseason run as the A's acquired Jeff Samardzija and Jason Hammel from the Chicago Cubs and ace Jon Lester along with Jonny Gomes from Boston. The moves failed to pay off as Oakland struggled down the stretch and barely held onto their playoff spot. Once in the postseason, Oakland blew a 7-3 lead in the eighth inning and an 8-7 edge in the 12th to lose 9-8 to the Kansas City Royals in the Wild Card game.

Coco Crisp #4 of the Oakland Athletics at Globe Life Park in Arlington on September 26, 2014, in Arlington, TX.

FIRST YEAR OF EXISTENCE: 1901
OWNER: LEW WOLFF AND JOHN J. FISHER
MANAGER: BOB MELVIN (JUNE 9, 2011-PRESENT)

PHILADELPHIA PHILLIES

The Philadelphia Phillies franchise has been a part of baseball since the 1883 season. The Phillies have not had much success on the field: they own just two World Series championships and seven National League pennants.

The franchise was dreadful in their first season as part of the NL. The Phillies finished just 17-81 on the season, losing their first game in franchise history on May 1, 1883, to the Providence Grays by a score of 4-3. The team posted its first winning mark in 1885, going 56-54, but a pennant was well off for the club.

The Phillies broke through with their first pennant in franchise history in 1915 but was defeated by Babe Ruth and the Boston Red Sox in five games in the World Series. The team finished second in the NL in 1916 and 1917 and followed that with 14 straight losing seasons from 1918 through 1931. The losing streak was halted in 1932 when Philadelphia went 78-76 and finished fourth. The team then strung together another 16 straight losing records, giving them 30 losing seasons in 31 years from 1918 to 1948.

Philadelphia claimed their second pennant in 1950 after winning 91 games. As it was in 1915, the World Series failed to go in the Phillies' favor, as they were swept by the New York Yankees. The team finished second in the 1964 season after blowing a 6.5-game lead with 12 games to play; a 10-game skid allowed the St. Louis Cardinals to steal the pennant.

The Phillies claimed three straight NL East titles between 1976 and 1978 but had no luck in the playoffs. The Reds swept the Phillies in 1976, while the Dodgers beat Philadelphia in four games in both 1977 and 1978. The Phillies returned to the playoffs in 1980 and defeated the Houston Astros in five games to advance to the World Series. Philadelphia claimed their first World Series championship with a six-game victory over the Kansas City Royals. The team returned to the World Series in 1983 but was beaten in five games by the Baltimore Orioles.

Philadelphia won the NL East in 1993, snapping a string of six consecutive losing seasons. The team claimed the NL pennant with a six-game victory over the Atlanta Braves in the NLCS, setting up a World Series matchup with the Toronto Blue Jays. Joe Carter's walk-off three-run home run in the bottom of the ninth inning in Game Six gave the Blue Jays their second consecutive World Series championship and left the Phillies disappointed once again.

The Phillies claimed the NL East title five years in a row from 2007 through 2011 and the team made a pair of World Series appearances. They defeated the Tampa Bay Rays in five games in 2008 to claim their second championship and were defeated by the Yankees in 2009 in six games. The team advanced to the NLCS in 2010, where they were downed by the San Francisco Giants in six games.

In 2011 the Phillies won the NL East for the fifth consecutive year, ringing up 102 regular season victories. The team was unable to fulfill their own expectations, dropping the NLDS to the St. Louis Cardinals in five games. The Phillies slipped from that 102-win campaign to a .500 season in 2012 as they finished 81-81 and missed the playoffs for the first time in five years.

Things went from bad to worse in 2013 as they Phillies went 73-89, 23 games out of first place.

Philadelphia fired manager Charlie Manuel on August 16, 2013, with the team standing 53-67. Ryne Sandberg was given the job on an interim basis, and the Phillies went 20-22 down the stretch. Following that, the team made the move to give him a three-year deal with an option for the 2017 season.

Philadelphia struggled throughout the 2014 season as expected, finishing 73-89 and in the basement of the NL East, 23 games behind the Washington Nationals. Cliff Lee made just 13 starts on the mound, hardly a return on the $25 million he was owed last season.

Ryan Howard #6 of the Philadelphia Phillies in action against the New York Mets at Citi Field on July 29, 2014 in the Flushing neighborhood of the Queens borough of New York City. The Phillies defeated the Mets 6-0.

FIRST YEAR OF EXISTENCE: 1883
OWNER: DAVID MONTGOMERY, GILES LIMITED PARTNERSHIP (BILL GILES), CLAIRE S. BETZ,
TRI-PLAY ASSOCIATES (WILLIAM C. BUCK), DOUBLE PLAY INC. (JOHN S. MIDDLETON)
MANAGER: RYNE SANDBERG (AUGUST 16, 2013-PRESENT)

MAJOR LEAGUE TEAMS

PITTSBURGH PIRATES

The Pittsburgh Pirates joined the American Association in 1882 and have been a part of the Major League Baseball scene since 1886 when they joined the National League. The club has won five World Series championships and nine NL pennants in the franchise's history.

The Pirates franchise played their first game on May 2, 1882, and recorded a 10-9 victory over the Cincinnati Red Stockings. The team finished 39-39 in their first season in the American Association. The club's best season in the AA, which came in 1886 when Pittsburgh finished 80-57, would be its last. The Pirates transitioned to the National League a year later and got off to a rough start as they finished 55-69 in 1887, the first of five straight losing seasons.

The Pirates didn't claim their first pennant until 1901. It was the first of three consecutive NL pennants for the franchise. Winning the pennant in 1903 allowed the Pirates to play in the first World Series in major league history against the Boston Americans; the Pirates lost the series, five games to three.

The team claimed its next pennant in 1909 and went on to win their first World Series championship. The Pirates won a franchise-record 110 games and defeated the Detroit Tigers in seven games to win the World Series. Babe Adams won three games for the Pirates and was the last rookie pitcher to win a Game Seven in the World Series for 93 years. The team didn't reach the World Series again until 1925, when they beat the Washington Senators to claim their second championship. The Pirates won the pennant in 1927 but were swept in the World Series by the Yankees and their "Murderer's Row" lineup.

It was 33 years before Pittsburgh claimed another pennant. The 1960 season saw Pittsburgh face the Yankees in the World Series. The Pirates won Games One, Four and Five by close scores, while the Yankees won Games Two, Three and Six by at least 10 runs. In the bottom of the ninth inning of Game Seven, Bill Mazeroski's walk-off solo home run gave Pittsburgh a 10-9 win and the title.

The Pirates made the playoffs five times in six years from 1970 to 1975 but had limited success, losing in the NLCS four times. In 1971 the Pirates beat the Baltimore Orioles in seven games to win the World Series. The team suffered tragedy on December 31, 1972, when outfielder Roberto Clemente was killed in a plane crash while accompanying a shipment of relief supplies to Nicaragua. In 1979 the Pirates and the Orioles clashed again in the World Series and Pittsburgh prevailed in seven games.

Pittsburgh dominated the NL East from 1990 through 1992 under manager Jim Leyland. With Barry Bonds, Bobby Bonilla, Doug Drabek and company, the team went to the NLCS in 1990, 1991 and 1992. Things didn't work out for the Pirates as they lost to the Cincinnati Reds in 1990 and to the Atlanta Braves in 1991 and 1992.

Pittsburgh finished 2011 with a record of 72-90, falling apart after the All-Star break. The team was 47-43 at the break but went 25-47 after it, cementing their 19th straight losing campaign. The Pirates melted down again in 2012. After leading the NL Central at the All-Star break for the first time since 1997, Pittsburgh faded down the stretch. The Pirates were 63-47 on August 8 but finished the season 79-83, their 20th consecutive losing season.

In 2013 the Pirates finished the year 94-68 and in second place in the NL Central to snap their string of losing seasons. They clinched a wild-card spot for their first playoff appearance since 1992. Pittsburgh beat Cincinnati 6-2 in the NL Wild Card game but was eliminated three games to two in the NLDS by the Cardinals.

Pittsburgh built on their momentum from 2013 as they posted back-to-back winning seasons for the first time since their three-year run from 1990-1992, finishing the year 88-74. Their season came to an abrupt end in the NL Wild Card game, however, as Madison Bumgarner of the San Francisco Giants shut the Pirates out by a score of 8-0.

Right fielder Roberto Clemente #21 of the Pittsburgh Pirates swings at the pitch during an MLB game circa 1968 at Three Rivers Stadium in Pittsburgh, PA.

FIRST YEAR OF EXISTENCE: 1882
OWNER: ROBERT NUTTING
MANAGER: CLINT HURDLE (NOVEMBER 14, 2010-PRESENT)

MAJOR LEAGUE TEAMS

SAN DIEGO PADRES

The San Diego Padres have been a part of Major League Baseball since the advent of divisional play in 1969. San Diego was one of four expansion teams to join the major league ranks that year, along with the Seattle Pilots, Montreal Expos and the Kansas City Royals.

The Padres were placed in the NL West, which is where they still reside today. The club played their first game on April 8, 1969, with a 2-1 victory over the Houston Astros before a crowd of 23,370. Things didn't go well the rest of the season, and San Diego finished 52-110 and was shut out 23 times.

The 1969 season was the first of nine consecutive losing seasons at the start of the franchise's history. San Diego failed to win more than 73 games in those nine seasons. The Padres' first winning season came in 1978 as the team went 84-78.

The Padres made their first playoff appearance in franchise history in 1984, winning the NL West with a record of 92-70 and then facing the Chicago Cubs in the NLCS. The Padres fell behind two games to none in the best-of-five series but rallied to win Games Three and Four to set up a winner-take-all Game Five. In that game, the Cubs led 3-0 after five innings but a crucial error by Cubs first baseman Leon Durham helped San Diego to a four-run inning. They prevailed 6-3 and captured the first NL pennant in team history. San Diego wasn't as fortunate in the World Series, as they lost in five games to a Detroit Tigers team that overpowered them.

San Diego didn't return to the postseason until 1996, when they claimed their second division title. They had no luck in the postseason, as the St. Louis Cardinals swept them in the NLDS to end their season. The team went from first in 1996 to last in 1997, dropping from 91 wins to 74 despite Tony Gwynn claiming his eighth NL batting title. Gwynn is tied with Honus Wagner for the most all time in the NL.

The Padres claimed the division in 1998 with a franchise-record 98 wins. In the playoffs, San Diego vanquished the Houston Astros three games to one in the NLDS and followed that up with a six-game defeat of the Atlanta Braves to claim their second pennant. The team ran out of magic in the World Series, as the talent-laden New York Yankees won the first of three straight titles, sweeping San Diego. Through the 2014 season, that marked the Padres' last trip to the World Series.

The team won the division in 2005 despite finishing with just an 82-80 record, but was swept in the Divisional Series by the Cardinals. The club claimed a second consecutive division title in 2006 but again was beaten by the Cardinals in the NLDS.

The Padres haven't made the playoffs since 2006. They struggled to finish 71-91 in 2011, despite some good performances from their starting pitching. Things didn't pan out well for San Diego in 2012 as they went 76-86 and finished in fourth place in the NL West. The rebuilding project continued on and off the field, and the Padres were sold for $800 million in August of that year.

The 2013 season wasn't much better for the team as they went 76-86, but they did manage to jump from fourth to third in the division. Entering the 2015 season, the Padres are the only team in the major leagues to never throw a no-hitter. They're one of two teams to never have a player hit for the cycle; the Marlins are the other.

San Diego finished the 2014 season with a 77-85 record for their fourth straight losing season. The team fired GM Josh Byrnes on June 22, and after six weeks with Omar Minaya as the interim GM, the team announced A. J. Preller as the team's GM on August 6. San Diego had major offensive struggles as they scored just 535 runs, which was last in the major leagues. They were fourth in runs allowed in the majors thanks to solid pitching and great defense. If the Padres had even an average offense, they would have been viable contenders. San Diego was last in the majors in runs, team batting average, on-base percentage and slugging percentage.

Starting pitcher Ian Kennedy #22 of the San Diego Padres delivers a pitch during the first inning against the Chicago Cubs at Wrigley Field on July 23, 2014, in Chicago, IL.

SAN DIEGO
19
FIRST YEAR OF EXISTENCE: 1969
OWNER: RON FOWLER
MANAGER: BUD BLACK (NOVEMBER 8, 2006-PRESENT)

MAJOR LEAGUE TEAMS

SAN FRANCISCO GIANTS

The San Francisco Giants have been a part of baseball since 1883 in the National League. They remained the New York Giants through 1957 when the team moved west to San Francisco. The Giants have claimed 23 NL pennants and eight World Series titles in franchise history. They have the second most World Series titles of NL teams; the Cardinals have the most with 11.

The club played its first game on May 1, 1883, and posted a 7-5 victory over the Boston Beaneaters. New York finished the year sixth in the league with a mark of 46-50. The team had its first winning season a year later, finishing 62-50.

The Giants won their first NL pennant in 1888 and their second pennant in 1889. The team was invigorated by the acquisition of John McGraw and several of his former players from Baltimore in 1902. The Giants won the pennant in 1904 but refused the opportunity to play in the World Series, as McGraw felt that the American League was inferior.

The Giants claimed a second consecutive pennant in 1905 and won their first title, defeating the Philadelphia A's in five games. The Giants won three straight pennants from 1911 to 1913 but Connie Mack's A's beat them in 1911 and 1913, while the Red Sox did the honors in 1912. The team returned to the World Series in 1917 but lost to the White Sox. McGraw's club won titles in 1921 and 1922, beating the Yankees both times. The Yankees and Washington Senators beat the Giants in the 1923 and 1924 World Series, respectively.

In 1933 the Giants won the NL pennant and took the World Series in five games over the Senators. Bill Terry guided the team to the pennant in 1936 and 1937, but the team lost to the Yankees in the World Series both years.

In 1951 the Giants rallied to force a three-game playoff with the Brooklyn Dodgers for the NL pennant. Bobby Thomson's three-run walk-off home run in Game Three gave the Giants the NL flag, but the powerhouse Yankees defeated them to claim the championship. In 1954 the Giants won their final championship in New York with a sweep of the Cleveland Indians.

The team relocated to San Francisco after the 1957 season and made the World Series for the first time on the West Coast in 1962 but fell to the Yankees. They returned to the World Series in 1989 but were swept by the Oakland A's.

With Barry Bonds in the lineup, the Giants made the World Series in 2002 and faced the Anaheim Angels. Despite Bonds hitting .471 with four home runs and 13 walks in the series, the Giants lost in seven games. In 2010 San Francisco beat the Texas Rangers in five games to win their first title since 1954. The Giants finished 86-76 in 2011, good for second place in the NL West.

The team was terrific in 2012, finishing the regular season 94-68to win the NL West. Catcher Buster Posey won the batting title with a .336 average and also won the NL MVP Award for his efforts.

The Giants beat the Reds in five games in the NLDS, rallying from a 2-0 series deficit to win. They advanced to the NLCS against the Cardinals. San Francisco trailed three games to one but outscored St. Louis 20-1 in the final three games. San Francisco swept the Tigers for their second championship in three years. In 2013 the team stumbled and finished 76-86 and in third place in the NL West.

In 2014 San Francisco finished the regular season 88-74 and earned a wild-card berth as they ended up six games behind the Dodgers. The Giants won the NL Wild Card game 8-0 over the Pittsburgh Pirates. San Francisco beat the Washington Nationals, three games to one, in the NLDS and followed that up with a five-game victory over St. Louis in the NLCS with Bumgarner being named NLCS MVP. In the World Series, the Giants defeated the Kansas City Royals in seven games; Bumgarner was named the MVP of the World Series after going 2-0 plus a save with a 0.43 ERA. He threw five innings on short rest in Game Seven, allowing no runs on two hits as the Giants won 3-2 for their third title in five years.

Madison Bumgarner #40 of the San Francisco Giants pitches against the Kansas City Royals in the fifth inning during Game Seven of the 2014 World Series at Kauffman Stadium on October 29, 2014, in Kansas City, MO.

FIRST YEAR OF EXISTENCE: 1883
OWNER: SAN FRANCISCO BASEBALL ASSOCIATED LP
MANAGER: BRUCE BOCHY (OCTOBER 27, 2006-PRESENT)

MAJOR LEAGUE TEAMS

SEATTLE MARINERS

The Seattle Mariners have been in Major League Baseball since 1977, when they were part of a team expansion in the American League. The team joined the AL at the same time as the Toronto Blue Jays. As of the 2014 season, the Mariners are one of only two current franchises in the major leagues without a pennant; the Washington Nationals are the other.

Seattle played the first game in franchise history on April 6, 1977, against the California Angels before a crowd of 57,762 at the Kingdome. The Mariners were blanked 7-0 by the Angels that night, as Frank Tanana beat Diego Segui. They would finish the 1977 season with a record of 64-98.

Losing was the trademark of the Mariners for the first part of their existence. They posted losing records in each of their first 14 seasons from 1977 to 1990, with three 100-loss campaigns to their credit. They posted their first winning season in 1991, Ken Griffey Jr.'s third year with the team, going 83-79.

Lou Piniella took over the managerial reins in 1993 and the Mariners began to improve. They posted their second winning season in franchise history that year, going 82-80, and after a down year in 1994 that was shortened by the strike, the Mariners claimed their first division championship in 1995. Seattle rallied from a 13-game deficit in mid-August to force a one-game playoff with the California Angels to decide the division championship. Randy Johnson outpitched Mark Langston, who the Mariners traded to get Johnson, and Seattle was victorious 9-1. After beating the New York Yankees in five games in the ALDS, Seattle was shut down by the Cleveland Indians in six games during the ALCS.

The Mariners returned to the postseason in 1997 after winning the AL West title but were stopped by the Baltimore Orioles in four games in the divisional round. Seattle made two more playoff appearances under Piniella in 2000 and 2001 but lost in the ALCS both years to the Yankees. The 2001 loss was disheartening for Mariners fans, who saw their team win an AL record 116 regular season games. What made that season more special was that Ken Griffey Jr. and Alex Rodriguez, the two superstars of the team for several years, were no longer part of the club, having both moved on.

The Mariners posted just four winning seasons in the 10 years spanning 2002 through 2011 and lost at least 93 games five times in that span. Seattle struggled in 2011, going just 67-95, though that was a six-game improvement over 2010. The 2012 campaign saw Seattle win 75 games, which was an eight-game improvement over their 2011 record. Kevin Millwood and five relievers tossed a no-hitter against the Dodgers on June 8. The Mariners tied a major league record by using six pitchers in a no-hitter; the 2003 Astros pulled off the same feat against the Yankees. Later in the season, on August 15, Felix Hernandez threw the first perfect game in franchise history as the Mariners blanked Tampa Bay 1-0 at Safeco Field.

Things didn't go any better for Seattle in 2013 as the team finished just 71-91. Thanks to the Houston Astros moving to the AL from the NL, Seattle avoided a fourth straight season in the cellar. They finished fourth instead but were 25 games behind the division winning A's. On September 27, Eric Wedge announced that he wouldn't be back with the team in 2014. Seattle did make a splash in free agency, signing Robinson Cano to a 10-year, $240 million deal to be an anchor in their lineup.

The 2014 season was better than expected for the Mariners, who finished the season with an 87-75 record and in the mix for a wild-card berth until the final weekend of the season before falling short. It was the team's first winning season since 2009. The team was part of the three-team deal with the Detroit Tigers and the Tampa Bay Rays that sent David Price to the Motor City. In the deal, the Mariners acquired Austin Jackson from Detroit and sent Nick Franklin to Tampa Bay.

Robinson Cano #22 of the Seattle Mariners is congratulated by third base coach Rick Donnelly #26 after hitting a solo home run against the Detroit Tigers.

FIRST YEAR OF EXISTENCE: 1977
OWNER: NINTENDO OF AMERICA (REPRESENTED BY HOWARD LINCOLN)
MANAGER: LLOYD MCCLENDON (NOVEMBER 7, 2013-PRESENT)

MAJOR LEAGUE TEAMS

ST. LOUIS CARDINALS

The St. Louis Cardinals have a long and storied pedigree, having played their first game in 1882. They have claimed 23 National League pennants and 11 World Series championships. Four of those pennants are from the team's years in the American Association. The Cardinals' 11 World Series titles are the most in NL history. They trail only the Yankees' 27 titles.

The 1882 season, when St. Louis was 37-43, marked the only losing season the franchise had in the AA. The team won four straight pennants from 1885 through 1888. Upon moving to the NL in time for the 1892 season, the franchise struggled and didn't finish higher than fourth until 1914.

The Cardinals hired Branch Rickey as the team's general manager in 1920. They claimed their first NL pennant in 1926 and then won the World Series to take their first championship, defeating the Yankees in seven games with help from a base-running miscue by Babe Ruth: down a run in Game Seven, Ruth was caught stealing to end the game. The team won the 1928 pennant but was swept by the Yankees. They returned to the Fall Classic in 1930 but lost to the Philadelphia A's in six games. They would beat the A's in seven games a year later. The Cardinals won it all in 1934 with a seven-game victory over the Detroit Tigers.

In 1942 the Cardinals won the pennant and defeated the Yankees in five games in the World Series, but in the 1943 Series they lost to the Yankees in five games. The 1944 World Series saw the Cardinals defeat the St. Louis Browns in six games, and in the 1946 Series St. Louis defeated the Boston Red Sox in seven games.

In 1964 the Philadelphia Phillies led by 6.5 games with 12 to play but lost 10 straight, allowing the Cardinals to win the pennant. St. Louis beat the Yankees in seven games to win the World Series. Behind Bob Gibson and Steve Carlton, the Cardinals won the World Series in seven games in 1967 over the Red Sox. Gibson had a 1.12 earned-run average in 1968 but the Cardinals fell in seven games to the Tigers.

In 1982 the Cardinals won the NL East and swept the Atlanta Braves in the NLCS before rallying from a three-games-to-two deficit to defeat the Milwaukee Brewers in the World Series. The Cardinals made the 1985 World Series but lost to the Kansas City Royals in seven games, in part due to a controversial call by Don Denkinger in the ninth inning of Game Six. The Cards never recovered.

In the 1987 World Series where the home team won all seven games, the Cardinals fell to the Minnesota Twins. St. Louis did not return to the playoffs until 1996, where they lost in seven games to the Braves in the NLCS. The Cardinals made the playoffs seven times between 2000 and 2009 but had just two World Series appearances. In those, they were swept by Boston in 2004 and beat Detroit in 2006.

In 2011 the Cardinals claimed the NL wild card with a late season surge coupled with Atlanta's swoon. The team edged the Phillies in the NLDS before beating the Brewers in six games in the NLCS. St. Louis rallied to defeat the Texas Rangers in seven games to claim the World Series.

St. Louis won 88 games in 2012 and was a wild-card team. The Cardinals eliminated Atlanta in the NL Wild Card game and recorded a 3-2 series win over the Washington Nationals in the NLDS to move on to the NLCS. The team took a 3-1 lead over the Giants but lost the final three games of the series. In 2013 St. Louis won 97 games and the NL Central. They beat the Pirates in the NLDS and claimed the NL pennant with a six-game series win over the Dodgers, but they lost the World Series in six games to the Red Sox.

In 2014 St. Louis repeated as champion of the NL Central as they went 90-72. The team defeated the Dodgers, three games to one, in the NLDS before being beaten in the NLCS in five games by the Giants. One of the Cardinals' top prospects, Oscar Taveras, was killed in a car accident in the Dominican Republic on October 26.

Ozzie Smith of the St. Louis Cardinals turns a double play during World Series game two between the St. Louis Cardinals and Milwaukee Brewers on October 13, 1982, at Busch Stadium in St. Louis, MO.

FIRST YEAR OF EXISTENCE: 1882
OWNER: WILLIAM DEWITT, JR., BILL HANSER AND KLINGAMAN GROUP
MANAGER: MIKE MATHENY (NOVEMBER 14, 2011-PRESENT)

MAJOR LEAGUE TEAMS

TAMPA BAY RAYS

The Tampa Bay Rays joined Major League Baseball in 1998 as part of baseball's most recent expansion. The Rays joined the AL East the same season as the Arizona Diamondbacks joined the NL West division. Originally known as the Devil Rays, the team became the Rays prior to the 2008 season. Tampa Bay has one AL pennant to their credit and is still seeking their first World Series championship.

The team's first pick in the expansion draft was Tony Saunders of the Florida Marlins. Tampa Bay struggled to a 63-99 record on the season, finishing in last place in the AL East. Wade Boggs picked up his 3000th career hit on August 7 of that year, hitting a home run to reach the mark.

The Rays had limited success over the following years, posting 10 consecutive losing seasons through 2007. During that time, Tampa Bay finished last in the division nine times, with a fourth-place finish in 2004 the only break in the monotony. The Rays failed to win more than 70 games in any season and posted three seasons where they lost at least 100 games. They went through Larry Rothschild, Hal McRae and Lou Piniella as managers before hiring Joe Maddon after the 2005 season. The club struggled in Maddon's first two seasons at the helm but got better as young talent developed.

Tampa Bay put together their first winning season in 2008, the year after they changed their franchise's name. They won a franchise-best 97 games that year and claimed their first AL East Division title. In the playoffs, Tampa Bay beat the Chicago White Sox in four games to advance to the ALCS. The Rays defeated the Boston Red Sox in seven games to clinch their first AL pennant. They advanced to the World Series but were defeated by the Philadelphia Phillies in five games. Through the 2014 season, it is the only World Series appearance for Tampa Bay in franchise history.

The club lost in the Division Series in five games to the Texas Rangers in 2010 after winning their second AL East title. The Rangers sunk Tampa Bay in the 2011 playoffs, this time in four games. That Tampa Bay made the playoffs in 2011 was a surprise in itself: the team rallied in September from a nine-game deficit to stun Boston. The Rays clinched the playoffs on the final day of the season, coming back from a 7-0 deficit in the eighth inning against the Yankees to win in 12 innings. Boston lost a 4-3 game to the Baltimore Orioles, giving up a pair of runs in the ninth inning to complete their collapse.

The 2012 season saw Tampa Bay ring up 90 victories on the season but end up third in the AL East, missing the playoffs. They made major changes in the offseason as they moved James Shields to Kansas City in a deal that brought back the Royals' top prospect, Wil Myers, as part of the package. David Price went 20-5 with a 2.56 ERA on the year and was the first Tampa Bay pitcher to win 20 games and claim the Cy Young Award.

In 2013 the Rays went 92-71 and finished second in the AL East, earning a wild-card berth. They dispatched the Indians in the AL Wild Card game, blanking the Tribe 4-0 to advance to the ALDS. Tampa Bay was knocked off by the eventual World Series champion, the Red Sox, three games to one. Myers was called up mid-season and hit .293 with 13 homers and 53 RBIs in 88 games and claimed the AL Rookie of the Year honors for his performance.

The 2014 campaign was a struggle for the Rays as they finished 77-85 for their first losing season since 2007. The team parted ways with Price, dealing him to the Detroit Tigers in a three-team trade that also included the Seattle Mariners. Tampa Bay received Drew Smyly and Willie Adames from Detroit plus Nick Franklin from Seattle.

Joe Maddon opted out of his contract and ended up taking over the managerial position with the Chicago Cubs. Andrew Friedman, who was the team's GM, took the job as president of baseball operations for the Los Angeles Dodgers. After an extended search, the Rays settled on Kevin Cash as the team's new manager on December 5.

Evan Longoria #3 of the Tampa Bay Rays connects on a ninth inning home run against the New York Yankees at Yankee Stadium on September 10, 2014, in the Bronx borough of New York City.

FIRST YEAR OF EXISTENCE: 1998
OWNER: STUART STERNBERG
MANAGER: KEVIN CASH (DECEMBER 5, 2014-PRESENT)

MAJOR LEAGUE TEAMS

TEXAS RANGERS

The Texas Rangers have been a part of Major League Baseball since the 1961 season, when the team was born as the Washington Senators. The Senators franchise was actually the second in the nation's capital with the name Senators. The previous incarnation moved in 1960 and became the Minnesota Twins. The league made the move to bring a team back to Washington in time for 1961 along with the Los Angeles Angels in an effort to avoid losing its antitrust exemption.

The franchise played its first game on April 10, 1961, before a crowd of 26,725 at Griffith Stadium. The rest of the season did not go so well for the team. After posting a 38-46 record at the All-Star break, the Senators went just 23-54 in the second half of the season to finish 61-100. It would mark the first of four straight 100-loss seasons to start the franchise's history and the first of eight straight losing seasons overall.

The Senators failed to finish better than sixth in the AL prior to the advent of divisional play and expansion in 1969. The team never won more than 76 games between 1961 and 1968. They posted their only winning season while in Washington during the 1969 campaign under Hall of Famer Ted Williams, going 86-76 in the newly formed AL East division.

After the 1971 season, the Senators up and left Washington again, as owner Bob Short tried to extract a $12 million sale price in order to keep the team in the nation's capital. When that failed to materialize (the Yankees were sold the same year for $8.8 million with a better fan base and track record), the die was cast for a move to be made. The team relocated to Arlington, Texas, in time for the 1972 season. The team's first game as the Rangers came on April 15, 1972, and lost 1-0 to the California Angels. The move did not lead to an immediate change in fortune as the Rangers lost 100-plus games in their first two seasons in Arlington.

The 1996 team won the AL West with a 90-72 record and made their first postseason appearance. Their trip to the playoffs would be short lived, as the Yankees beat the Rangers in four games. That season marked the first of three division titles in four years between 1996 and 1999. The Rangers had limited success in the playoffs despite winning in the regular season. They were swept in the divisional round in both 1998 and 1999, both times at the hands of the Yankees.

Texas claimed the 2010 AL West championship and won the first postseason series in franchise history when they eliminated the Tampa Bay Rays in four games during the ALDS. The Rangers proceeded to capture their first AL pennant with a six-game win over their postseason nemesis, the Yankees. The Rangers' good fortune ended there, as the San Francisco Giants claimed their first World Series title since 1954, beating the Rangers in five games.

Texas repeated as AL West champions in 2011. The team faced the Rays in the divisional round and eliminated Tampa Bay in four games. In the ALCS, Texas handled the Detroit Tigers in six games, claiming their second consecutive AL pennant. Texas fell short in the World Series, blowing two chances in Game Six to put St. Louis away, and was defeated in Game Seven.

The Rangers won 93 games in 2012 and were second in the AL West behind the A's. The team made the playoffs as a wild-card team. Things didn't go the Rangers' way in the postseason as they were knocked off by 5-1 by the Orioles in the AL Wild Card game. In 2013 the Rangers ended up winning 91 games but finished 5.5 games behind the A's for the AL West crown but missed the postseason. Nolan Ryan stepped down as CEO of the team on October 31, 2013.

The 2014 season was one that the Rangers would rather forget rather than remember. They finished the year with a 67-95 mark and in the basement of the AL West. Ron Washington resigned as manager on September 5; Tim Bogar went 14-8 as the interim manager but wasn't asked back. On October 16, the Rangers named Jeff Banister the team's manager.

Ivan Rodriguez #7 of the Texas Rangers throws the ball back to the pitcher during the game against the Cleveland Indians at Progressive Field on September 9, 2009, in Cleveland, OH. The Rangers defeated the Indians 10-0.

Wilson
FIRST YEAR OF EXISTENCE: 1961
OWNER: RAY DAVIS, BOB SIMPSON
MANAGER: JEFF BANISTER (OCTOBER 16, 2014-PRESENT)

MAJOR LEAGUE TEAMS

TORONTO BLUE JAYS

The Toronto Blue Jays have been in Major League Baseball since 1977 and were part of a two-team expansion in the American League. The Seattle Mariners joined the AL at the same time as the Blue Jays, who were the second Canadian franchise in the majors, following the Montreal Expos. The Blue Jays have won a pair of AL pennants and claimed the World Series in both pennant-winning years of the franchise.

The Blue Jays played the inaugural game in franchise history on April 7, 1977, in a home game at Exhibition Stadium against the Chicago White Sox. Toronto's happy days were few and far between in 1977, as the team finished 54-107 despite winning three of the first four and five of the first seven games in franchise history.

The Blue Jays posted three consecutive 100-loss seasons to start their history, including a franchise-record 109 defeats in the 1979 season. The team improved to just 95 losses in 1980, was 37-69 in the strike-shortened 1981 season and then finished 78-84 in 1982. It was the first time in the franchise's six-year existence they did not finish last.

The Blue Jays captured their first AL East championship in 1985 and made their first postseason appearance after winning a franchise-record 99 games. Unfortunately for Toronto, they ran into a tough Kansas City Royals team, who doused the Blue Jays' championship hopes with a five-game victory in the ALCS.

The team strung together 11 consecutive winning seasons from 1983 to 1993, making five playoff appearances during that span. Toronto narrowly missed the playoffs in 1987. After leading the Detroit Tigers by one game with three to go, the Blue Jays were swept by the Tigers on the final weekend of the season. George Bell was named the AL MVP after hitting .308 with 47 home runs and 134 RBIs. Toronto returned to the playoffs in 1989, winning the division. The team was vanquished in the ALCS, however, as the Oakland A's beat Toronto in five games.

The Blue Jays had three straight 90-win seasons from 1991 through 1993, making the playoffs each time as the AL East champion. In 1991 the team fell short of the World Series as they dropped a five-game series to the Minnesota Twins. Toronto returned to the playoffs in 1992 and claimed the team's first pennant with a six-game victory over the A's. In the World Series, the Blue Jays beat the Atlanta Braves in six games to claim their first World Series crown and the first by a Canadian team in history. Toronto repeated as AL champions in 1993 after besting the Chicago White Sox in six games, setting up a matchup with the Philadelphia Phillies in the Fall Classic. Joe Carter's walk-off three-run homer in the bottom of the ninth inning off Mitch Williams in Game Six gave the Blue Jays an 8-6 victory and their second consecutive World Series victory.

The 1993 title was the last time through 2014 that the Blue Jays won the World Series or even played for it; Toronto hasn't made the postseason since that season. The Blue Jays finished the 2011 season with an 81-81 record, good for fourth in the AL East.

Toronto had a miserable 2012 campaign as they finished the year with a 73-89 mark and another fourth-place finish in the AL East. The Blue Jays used a franchise-record 34 pitchers during the course of the year and had to battle injuries all season long.

The offseason leading into the 2013 season was a busy one for Toronto. Their manager, John Farrell, was moved to the Red Sox and promptly led Boston to a World Series title. To replace him, Toronto brought John Gibbons back for a second tour of duty with the franchise. Despite all their acquisitions, things didn't pan out for them. The Blue Jays finished the season 74-88 and ended up in last place in the AL East.

Toronto had a better season in 2014 as they finished the year 83-79 and in third place in the AL East, 13 games off the pace in the division. The Blue Jays led the division for most of the first couple months of the season but faded down the stretch.

Jose Bautista #19 of the Toronto Blue Jays connects on a seventh inning home run against the New York Yankees at Yankee Stadium on September 20, 2014 in the Bronx borough of New York City.

FIRST YEAR OF EXISTENCE: 1977
OWNER: ROGERS COMMUNICATIONS
MANAGER: JOHN GIBBONS (NOVEMBER 20, 2012-PRESENT)

WASHINGTON NATIONALS

The Washington Nationals have been in Major League Baseball since 1969. That year brought four new teams to the sport and the advent of divisional play. Along with the Nationals (who were then known as the Montreal Expos), the Seattle Pilots, Kansas City Royals and the San Diego Padres also joined. The Pilots, who would become the Milwaukee Brewers in 1970, and the Royals would play in the American League, while the Expos and Padres took up residence in the National League. The Expos were the first team in Major League Baseball history to be based in Canada.

The franchise played the first game in its history on April 8, 1969, on the road at Shea Stadium in New York against the Mets. Like most expansion teams, there were few bright spots for the team in its first year and Montreal finished 52-110, 48 games out of first.

Montreal posted 95 victories in 1979 but failed to make the postseason as they finished two games behind the Pittsburgh Pirates, who went on to win the World Series. In 1981, led by catcher Gary Carter, along with outfielders Andre Dawson and Tim Raines, the Expos won the first division title in franchise history, capturing the second half title in the NL East.

The 1981 season was shortened by the strike, forcing teams to play two halves of a season. In the NL Division Series, the Expos defeated the Philadelphia Phillies in five games to set up a NL Championship Series matchup with the Los Angeles Dodgers. With the best-of-five series tied at two games apiece and Game Five deadlocked at 1 in the ninth inning, Rick Monday's solo home run off Steve Rogers was the difference in a 2-1 Dodger win and the NL pennant.

The franchise has not been that close since. The Expos had the best record in the NL in 1994 when the strike hit, wiping out the rest of the season. They were slated for contraction after a vote in 2001 along with the Minnesota Twins but an injunction forcing the Twins to play in the Metrodome during the 2002 year ended those talks.

Major League Baseball, who owned the Expos after buying them from Jeffrey Loria, looked for possible relocation sites for the team. In 2003 and 2004 the Expos played 22 of their home games in San Juan, Puerto Rico. On September 29, 2004, Major League Baseball announced that the Expos would relocate to Washington, D.C., in time for the 2005 season.

The club strung together six straight losing seasons from 2006 through 2011, losing 100 or more games twice in that span and at least 90 games two other times. Washington finished the 2011 season 80-81, with Davey Johnson taking over from manager Jim Riggleman in late June after Riggleman resigned because he was unable to negotiate a contract extension.

In 2012 things all started to fall in place for the Nationals. Washington won a franchise-record 98 games en route to the NL East title. Despite their success, the Nationals stuck to the plan of limiting Strasburg's innings as he recovered from Tommy John surgery that cut his 2011 season short and shut him down after 159.1 innings. As it turned out, his absence from the rotation may have been an issue. Washington dropped the NLDS, three games to two, to St. Louis. The Nationals held a 6-0 lead after three innings in Game Five and led 7-5 in the ninth, but the Cardinals got four runs off Drew Storen and the Nationals feel-good season was over.

The Nationals didn't have the same sort of success in 2013. The team posted an 86-76 record, giving them winning records in back-to-back seasons for the first time since 2002 and 2003 but they finished 10 games behind the Braves in the division and missed the playoffs.

The 2014 season saw the Nationals return to the top of the NL East as they finished the season 96-66. They were the lone team in the division above .500 as they cruised to a 17-game margin in the standings at season's end. In the postseason, Washington fizzled out as they were defeated three games to one by the San Francisco Giants in the NLDS.

Stephen Strasburg #37 of the Washington Nationals pitches against the Arizona Diamondbacks at Nationals Park on August 19, 2014, in Washington, DC.

FIRST YEAR OF EXISTENCE: 1969
OWNER: LERNER ENTERPRISES
MANAGER: MATT WILLIAMS (OCTOBER 31, 2013-PRESENT)

PENCE
BASEBALL CLUB

SAN FRANCISCO
GIANTS
BASEBALL CLUB

RUCKUS
BOOKS

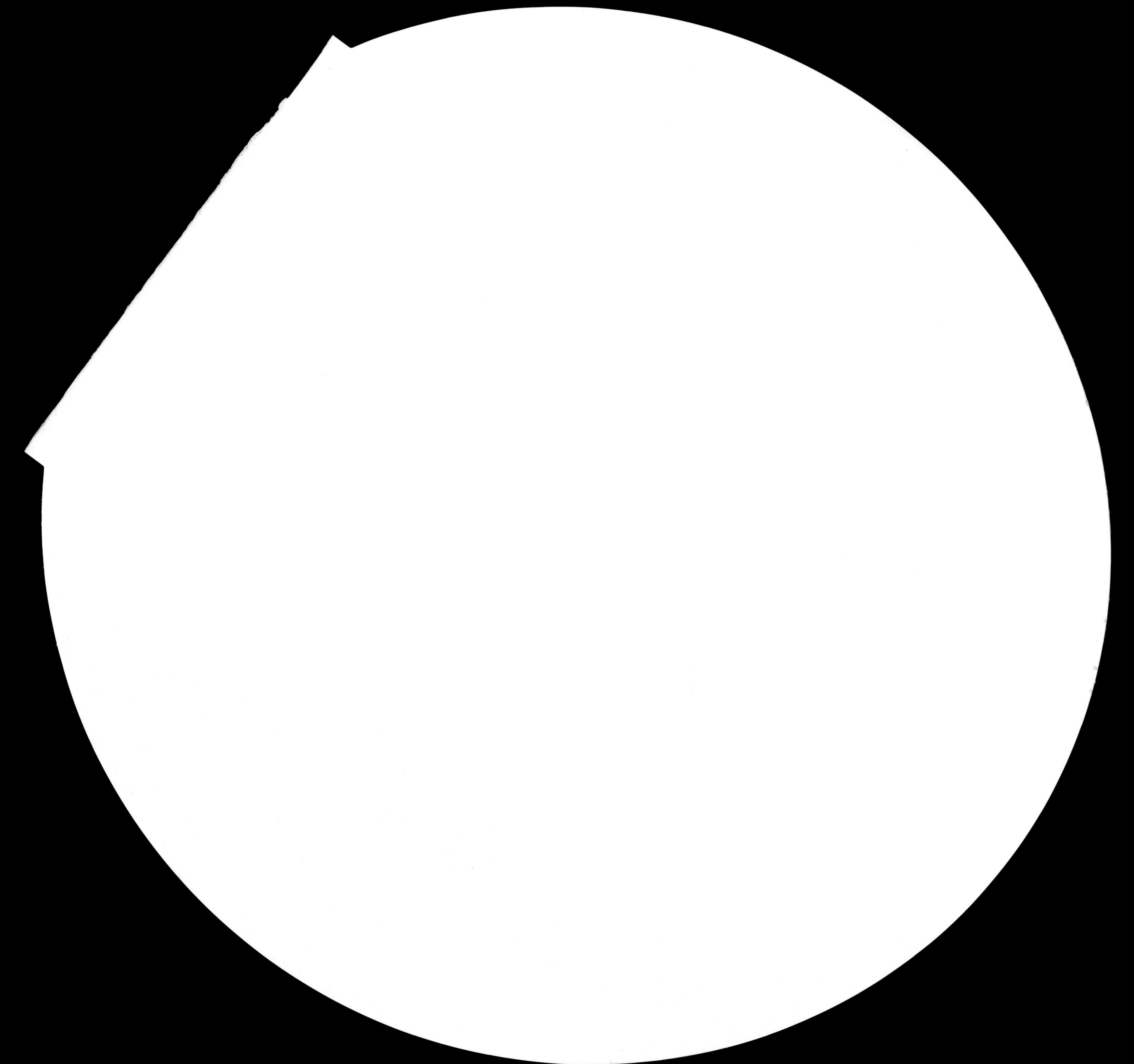

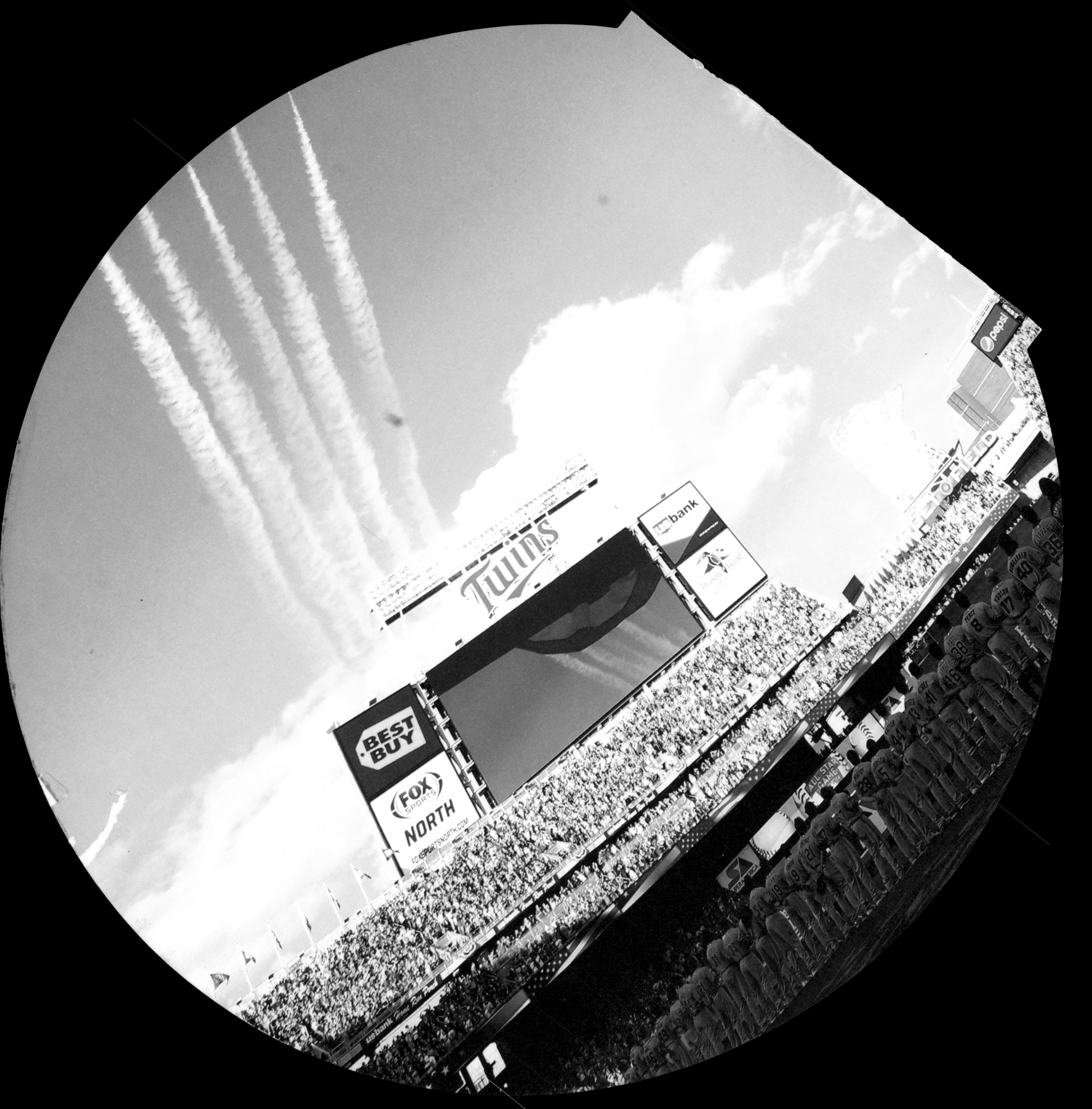
BEST BUY
FOX SPORTS
NORTH
FOXSPORTSNORTH.COM
Twins
bank
pepsi